New Ways in Using Communicative Games in Language Teaching

Nikhat Shameem and Makhan Tickoo, Editors

New Ways in TESOL Series II
Innovative Classroom Techniques
Jack C. Richards, Series Editor

Founded 1966

Teachers of English to Speakers of Other Languages, Inc.

Typeset in Garamond Book and Tiffany Demi
by Capitol Communication Systems, Inc., Crofton, Maryland USA
and printed by
Pantagraph Printing, Bloomington, Illinois USA

Teachers of English to Speakers of Other Languages, Inc. (TESOL)
1600 Cameron Street, Suite 300
Alexandria, VA 22314 USA
Tel 703-836-0774 • Fax 703-836-7864 • e-mail: tesol@tesol.edu • http://www.tesol.edu/

Director of Communications and Marketing: Helen Kornblum
Managing Editor: Marilyn Kupetz
Copy Editors: Betsy Kelaher and Marcia Annis
Cover Design: Ann Kammerer

ISBN 939791-78-1
Library of Congress Catalogue No. 98-061416

Contents

Acknowledgments

Thanks go to all the people around the world who contributed to this book, giving other people involved in the wide field of learning and teaching English as an additional language (EAL) many more useful and enjoyable ideas for using English communicatively.

In particular, I would like to thank my coeditor, Makhan Tickoo, for sharing this project with me and disseminating information about this publication so extensively that we received such a broad variety of submissions from teachers all over the world. I am also grateful to my friends in the field of applied linguistics who so thoughtfully geared their submissions toward the sections in the book that needed more activities.

I would especially like to thank Anit Singh and my parents, Abdul Azeez and Ayesha Shameem, for their patience and understanding while I spent much of my leave and free time over Christmas working on this project.

Nikhat Shameem

Introduction

This book is primarily about communication and addresses the very important role of language in society. Students who learn English as an additional language (EAL) already have highly developed skills in their own language—skills that can be transferred and applied to the learning of a new language. Communicative activities play an essential role in teaching English in that they allow students to use strategies in realistic situations akin to those for which they would use their L1.

Communicative activities are therefore particularly suited to beginners who may not have a comfortable command of the structures of the English language or intermediate- and advanced-level students who have good literacy skills in their L1 and L2 but need support in developing their interpersonal communication skills and fluency. By introducing a competitive element and presenting the activity as a game, students develop communication skills incidentally. A retrospective look at the game and its purpose might be a valuable addition to many of the activities contained in this book.

Use of Communicative Games

We believe that the goal of language learning is communication. The goal of language teaching is therefore teaching students to communicate in the language they are learning so that they can use it successfully to perform a variety of functions. Learning will take place consciously if students perceive a need for it. For example, if students have only learned English to pass an examination, then the language they might have acquired is probably transitional and focused on that needed for the test. Communicative games give language learning a whole new meaning. Learning takes place—even if incidentally—while the students are engaged in a self-motivating activity. They are having fun and interacting socially (in pairs, in small groups, or with the whole class) to perform a task and reach a satisfactory outcome. Although the classroom can never be representative of all authentic real-life situations, it nevertheless represents a "real social context in its own right" (Littlewood, 1981, p. 44).

Nation and Thomas (1988) point out that the most effective learning takes place when there are challenges involved. In most of the activities in this book, authors have suggested ways to cater their activities to different levels so that the same activity can be used repeatedly and made more difficult at successive tries. Many involve competition and challenge students to complete a task in a limited time. However, competition might not be the best motivation for students who are not used to this concept in their own culture; in this case, an activity emphasizing information sharing might be more effective.

The activities in this book are from a variety of authors with differing social and linguistic backgrounds. As such they present a unique blend of communicative games that have been used successfully in language classrooms globally. It is important that teachers select the tasks that are most suited to their students' needs, considering their purpose for using English and the context in which they will use it.

It is also important that students perceive communicative activities as a legitimate learning strategy. Positive attitudes to learning activities are essential if the desired outcome is to be achieved. Therefore, the rationale behind the use of communicative games in language classrooms needs to be explained and justified because the goals of these activities might not be apparent merely by participation.

Classifying the Tasks

Below is an overview of the rationale used in selecting and sorting the tasks in this book. The classification, using the five general goals of communicative activities, was taken from Nation and Thomas (1988). The five parts have been arranged to reflect the main goals of communicative activities in their order of usefulness to students:

Part I: Learning Communication Strategies
Part II: Learning Content Matter

The Goals of Communicative Activities

Learning communication strategies is identified as a primary task because the goal of communication is the least threatening aspect of language learning. It is also the first strategy that students will need—language for basic communication. This is critical in a variety of situations for such beginners as new immigrants, international students, and refugees, who are adjusting socially and linguistically to a new environment.

Learning the content matter is second in terms of usefulness in the powerful context of language across the curriculum. Students are using English, which is not their L1, to access subject area content that they must master to achieve compatible educational standards with their native-English-speaking peers. Being effective language users in the mainstream means that EAL students have access to mainstream educational opportunities and knowledge.

Research shows that new language items can be learned incidentally and effectively when students participate in communication activities. Students learn new items from the nature of the task and from each other. In mixed ability groups in particular, less proficient students benefit in their language learning from working with more proficient peers (Kessler, 1992; Nunan, 1992). Although there are many activities here for learning and practicing new language, it is important that these activities be seen as part of the broader communicative framework. The framework of a communicative activity allows for the meaningful and contextualized learning of new language items and structures as well as the practice of old ones. This permits attention to appropriateness, fluency, and correctness.

In learning skills in discourse, students are putting together the language they have acquired to form meaningful units. Working on collaborative stories, for example, allows students to use the strategies they have learned to manipulate their content knowledge and collaboratively construct a coherent story. If they used several different media to retell the stories or retold them to several interlocutors—particularly over a decreasing time frame, they would become more fluent.

Learning new language items and discourse skills is important for students at the beginning and intermediate levels, and it is essential that they have plenty of opportunities to revise and consolidate new learning to reach the advanced level.

The five parts of this book, therefore, cover the five main goals of communicative activities in language teaching and learning. Each of these parts is divided into skill areas targeted within each goal. The activities in the final section provide fluency practice in a range of language and skill areas. Teachers can choose tasks according to the main goal of the lesson and the skill area they wish to address. Within each section the activities are sorted by level, and each section begins with activities that would work at any level.

References and Further Reading

Kessler, C. (Ed). (1992). *Co-operative language learning: A teacher's resource book.* Englewood Cliffs, NJ: Prentice Hall.

Littlewood, W. (1981). *Communicative language teaching: An introduction.* Cambridge: Cambridge University Press.

Nation, I. S. P., & Thomas, G. I. (1988). *Communication activities.* (Occasional Paper No. 13). Wellington, New Zealand: English Language Institute, Victoria University of Wellington.

Nunan, D. (1992). *Collaborative language learning and teaching.* Cambridge: Cambridge University Press.

Users' Guide to Activities

Part III: Learning From One Another

Enriching Vocabulary and Productive Use

Imparting and Seeking Factual Information

Confirmation and Clarification

Expressing Emotional Attitudes

Part IV: Developing Skills in Discourse

Conducting Interviews and Conversations

Collaborative Storytelling: Speaking

Sharpening Speaking

Working With Writing

Part I: Learning Communication Strategies

Editors' Note

Knowledge of communication strategies empowers individuals to communicate, express themselves, perform many different functions, and attain satisfactory outcomes. Above all, knowing the possible strategies they can use allows learners to make up for any lack of language knowledge and ensures more effective communication.

In this section, contributors offer activities that concentrate primarily on helping students recognize and use communicative strategies to facilitate functional communication and interaction in an L2 in realistic everyday contexts. To practice effective and accurate communication, some formulaic expressions and repair strategies are used. This section is divided into three key areas: asking questions for clarification or information; negotiating meaning or negotiating in the context of buying and selling; practicing pronunciation to enhance listening comprehension.

◆ Asking Questions
Beat the Ball

Levels
Beginning +

Aims
Learn the names of
classmates in a relaxed
environment
Ask simple questions
and practice useful
expressions

Class Time
Variable

Preparation Time
Enough to find a ball or
similar object

Resources
Soft ball

This is a good introductory activity to use in a first class when students need to learn each others' names. It involves basic personal communication at a simple level. You can even create the soft ball from scrunched paper, making this activity as easy for you as it is useful for students.

Procedure

1. Seat the students so that they can all see each other (e.g., in a horseshoe shape or circle). Explain that the purpose of the game is to learn the names of class members.
2. Explain how to play the game: One student must call a classmate's name and then throw the ball to that person; all students need to listen so they know when to catch the ball.
3. The game will proceed slowly at first because students will not know each other's names. In this case they must ask a question, such as, "What's your name please?" "What was your name again?" "I'm sorry, I've forgotten your name; could you tell me again, please?" Encourage the students not to throw to the same student every time so that they learn as many names as possible.
4. Students should not throw the ball just to their friends or people near them. They must ask any necessary questions and call a student's name before throwing the ball, making it clear that the ball is meant for that student.
5. Play the game for as long as you feel necessary. During the first week of class spend the first few minutes of each class period playing the game.

Caveats and Options

1. It is important for students to include the teacher so that they can learn the teacher's name and feel that the teacher is part of the group.
2. Depending on the level of the students and how quickly they pick up the game, you can adapt it to include other structures (e.g., *the person sitting on the right of Sumiko*, *the person next to Juan*, *the person opposite me*).
3. Because this is a warm-up activity, it may be played at any time to build students' fluency and speed with sentences, questions, or words. The teacher or another student throws the ball, and the recipient must utter the sentence, phrase, or answer before catching the ball.

Contributor

Sarah Berg, originally from Australia, is currently teaching in Tokyo, Japan, where she has been living and working since 1988.

Who Am I?

Levels
Beginning–intermediate

Aims
Practice forming and
using interrogatives

Class Time
15 minutes

Preparation Time
None

Resources
Small strips of paper
and safety pins

Because interrogatives are a high-frequency construction in communicative language exchange, it is useful to give students at beginning and low intermediate levels as much practice as possible in forming and producing them. This game provides students with intensive practice in using interrogatives while avoiding the monotony of mechanical drills.

Procedure

1. Each student thinks of the name of a well-known personality, living or dead, whom they would expect the whole class to know. The student writes the name on a piece of paper and folds the paper.
2. Collect all the names in a box. Shake the box and ask each student to pull out a paper. Tell the students not to unfold the paper.
3. Distribute one safety pin to each of the students. Make sure that the students do not select the paper they put into the box.
4. Put students into pairs, naming one partner A and the other B. Tell A to pin B's paper with the name to B's back. B must not know this name. Repeat this previous step, telling B to pin A's paper with the name to A's back.
5. Ask A to try to guess the name pinned on A's back by asking B questions in the first person (e.g., "Am I a man or a woman?" "Am I dead or alive?" "Am I a famous singer?" "Have you ever seen me on television?").
6. Have B use the same process to find out the name pinned on B's back.
7. Ask students to take off their name papers, put them back in the box, and repeat the procedure.

Caveats and Options

1. Other names, such as those of countries, can be used instead of those of famous people (e.g., "Am I a large or a small country?" "Am I in Asia?" "Is the main religion in my country Buddhism?" "Is my capital Tokyo?").
2. Limits can be imposed, such as a time limit of 5 minutes or a limited number of questions (e.g., 20 questions).
3. If the class is in a monocultural setting, students can be asked to think of national personalities. For example, for a class of Hong Kong students, personalities could be local pop singers, such as Andy Lau, or politicians, such as Martin Lee. For multicultural classes the personalities should be of widely known international stature (e.g., William Shakespeare, Michael Jackson, Mahatma Gandhi).

Contributor

Dino Mahoney is an associate professor in the English Department of the City University of Hong Kong. He also has taught ESL/EFL in England, Greece, and the United Arab Emirates.

Unmasking a Celebrity

Levels
High beginning +

Aims
React spontaneously to
questions from
classmates
Formulate impromptu
follow-up questions

Class Time
Variable

Preparation Time
3 minutes per character

Resources
Index cards
Plastic bag
Chalkboard or
whiteboard with chalk
or markers, or overhead
projector (OHP) with an
overhead transparency
(OHT) and a marker

This warm-up activity is student- and task-centered. Students will learn to focus on themselves and others as well as the problem they have to solve—namely, guessing the name of a famous celebrity or popular person. By reacting to each others' questions, answers, and hints, students develop effective strategies for finding a solution.

Procedure

1. Distribute two index cards per student. Ask students to write the names of four popular or famous persons (e.g., writers, sports figures, politicians, singers, actors, scientists, cartoon characters, or people well known on campus or in the local community), one each on the front and back of both index cards.
2. Collect all of the index cards in a plastic bag.
3. Explain the game, telling students that one of them has to leave the room while the rest (as a group) draw a name from the bag. The student who left the room is called back into the class and tries to guess the name of the famous person by asking the other students questions.
4. Ask one student to leave the room.
5. Ask two other students to select a name from the bag. Have one of them hold the bag while the other one draws an index card.
6. Take the index card and quickly choose one of the names written on the front or back of the card. Write the name on the chalkboard, whiteboard, or OHT so that everybody in the class can see it. Then wipe the board clean or turn off the OHP.
7. Ask the student who left the room to return and ask the class three initial questions which require yes or no answers.

8. Tell the student guessing the name to ask five additional follow-up questions to help unmask the identity of the famous or popular person.
9. Ask the class to respond to these questions by giving the person guessing hints or details using key words or whole sentences about the popular or famous person.
10. The student guessing may say the solution (i.e., the name of the popular or famous person) at any time.
11. The game is over when the student correctly guesses the name of the person on the card or, after asking the five follow-up questions, fails to unmask the identity of the person.
12. In either event, turn on the OHP and reveal the name or write it on the chalkboard or whiteboard.

References and Further Reading

Angelo, T. A., & Cross, K. (1993). *Classroom assessment techniques: A handbook for college teachers*. San Francisco: Jossey-Bass.

Contributor

Claudia Becker teaches intermediate and advanced academic writing classes for international students as well as tests and places students in the English as a Second and International Language Program at Loyola University Chicago. Her research areas include free writing in the initial stages of foreign language acquisition, sociolinguistic aspects of German in the work place, and spoken versus written language proficiency.

Family Feud With Errata Cards

Levels
High beginning +

Aims
Recognize own mistakes
in speech
Monitor speech or
writing for accuracy

Class Time
30 minutes

Preparation Time
1 hour, initially

Resources
Collection of sentences
containing common
student errors

This competitive error correction game helps students to teach each other and breaks down barriers to peer evaluation. Because the errors belong to no one, students feel free to criticize openly and offer suggestions without worrying about hurting one another's feelings.

Procedure

1. Collect a list of errors common to your students or errors that review or reinforce a grammar point that you have been studying (see Appendix).
2. Print the list on cards, with each card containing one sentence. (The game works best when each sentence contains only one error.)
3. Separate the class into teams.
4. Have one member of each team approach the teacher's podium or desk.
5. Show the sentence with the error to both students. The student who thinks she can correct the sentence hits the teacher's desk and attempts the correction. If correct, the student's team receives a point. If incorrect, the opportunity to correct the error passes to the student from the second team.
6. If both players fail to correct the sentence, they must hit the table again for a chance to correct the sentence. If the delay is too long, you can open the sentence to the class to see if anyone can correct it. The team that succeeds in correcting the sentence scores half a point.
7. The game ends when all cards are finished. The team with the most points wins.

Caveats and Options

1. Errors must be appropriate to the level of the students. If they are too easy or too difficult, students will lose interest.
2. Take time to explain difficult errors. It stretches the game and gives students a break from standing up and sitting down.

References and Further Reading

Azar, S. B. (1990). *Understanding and using English grammar*. Englewood Cliffs, NJ: Prentice Hall.

Rinvolucri, M. (1984). *Grammar games*. Cambridge: Cambridge University Press.

Appendix: Sample Errors

That is ugly dog.
I want to visit in Tokyo.
Can you play the ski?
Japan and Korea is very different.
She is carefully about speaking English.
I like dog more than cat.
I have five family.
Canada is big country.
Why happened the accident?

Contributor

Kelly E. Quinn teaches English in Nagoya, Japan.

What Is It?

Levels
Intermediate +

Aims
Practice asking
questions
Develop deductive
reasoning skills
Review vocabulary

Class Time
20–30 minutes

Preparation Time
5 minutes

Resources
One small piece of
paper, with one
vocabulary item, per
person
Tape and scissors

This activity is an enjoyable way to practice asking questions while developing deductive reasoning skills and revising vocabulary. It is adapted from a common party game.

Procedure

1. Have the students sit in a circle facing one another. Give each student a piece of paper with a vocabulary item on it and a small piece of tape.
2. Have each student stick the paper on another student's forehead, with the word facing outward so that the person cannot see the word but everyone else can.
3. Taking turns, allow the students 1 or 2 minutes to ask questions to guess their word.

Caveats and Options

1. An alternative to the 1- or 2-minute time limit is to change the person asking questions after that person has gotten three incorrect answers.
2. Rather than writing the words before class, with more advanced levels, you can simply hand out blank pieces of paper and have students write the words themselves.

Graeme Smith is teaching in Auckland, New Zealand, and has just completed an MA in language teaching at the University of Auckland.

Contributor

◆ Negotiating Shadow Tableaux

Levels
Beginning–intermediate

Aims
Practice speculating and using various modal forms

Class Time
10 minutes

Preparation Time
None

Resources
Overhead projector (OHP)

Expressing uncertainty and speculating are high-frequency language functions. This game enables students to generate the language of speculation and practice various modal forms in an enjoyable, nonthreatening environment.

Procedure

1. Pass around a bag and ask students to put something personal in it (e.g., lipstick, a penknife, a novelty key ring, a scarf, a badge). Add a few more unusual items to the bag yourself (e.g., a thimble, a chess piece, some rice, a glove).
2. Count the number of items. Tip the bag of items onto the glass top of an OHP. Allow the items to tumble out in a random fashion.
3. Place a card or book in front of the OHP so that the students cannot see the items on it.
4. Switch on the OHP. The jumbled silhouettes of the collected items will be projected onto a screen or whiteboard.
5. Tell the students the number of items on the OHP, explaining that the aim of the game is to guess as many of them as possible.
6. Elicit speculation on three or four of the items.
7. Ask students to continue working in pairs or threes to come to an agreement on what they believe the objects to be. Have them make a list of the items.
8. Ask the pair or group with the highest number of listed items to read them out loud.

Caveats and Options

1. If the items you collect all seem rather obvious, you may increase the chance of speculation by grouping them on the OHP in a more difficult way by overlapping them or adjusting the focus on the OHP so that the silhouettes of the objects are blurred.

2. Preteach ways of speculating and various modal forms appropriate to the level of your class, for example:

   I'm not sure but I think it's a . . .
   It might be a . . .
   It could be a . . .
   It looks like a . . .

3. Monitor the class and be prepared to help students with vocabulary, particularly with low-frequency words.

4. This game is also useful for teaching vocabulary, particularly word sets. At the beginning level, for example, shadow tableaux can be made of various fruits and vegetables (e.g., a banana, mushroom, cherry, spring onion, eggplant, mango, kiwi fruit, watercress).

Contributor

Dino Mahoney is an associate professor in the English Department of the City University of Hong Kong. He also has taught ESL/EFL in England, Greece, and the United Arab Emirates.

Pop Quiz

Levels
Intermediate +

Aims
Improve speaking and
reading comprehension
skills

Class Time
5–10 minutes for whole-
class work
10–15 minutes for pair
work

Preparation Time
1 hour

Resources
Multiple-choice quiz
based on information
from an almanac or any
quantifiable quiz

Caveats and Options

Pop Quiz is an instrument that creates deliberate information and opinion gaps among foreign language learners. These gaps are filled through cooperative action. Critical thinking and problem solving are encouraged. Heated discussions may take place on some real-world issues, especially on controversial ones. This activity allows students to use language freely and without the constraints of typical classroom exercises. Depending on the students' level of proficiency, there is heavy or little reliance on their referent.

Procedure

1. Select items from an almanac or choose any quantifiable piece of information; if necessary, translate it into the target language.
2. Write three distractors and the correct answer (see Appendix) and create the quiz.
3. Have students take the pop quiz, discuss their answers in pairs, and try to reach an agreement.
4. Provide the answers.
5. Have students discuss in pairs and with you whether they were surprised by the answer and why, and why their guesses were higher or lower than the actual figure.

1. Depending on the sensitivity of a social issue and the ideologies of the participants, certain topics, such as abortion and gun control, should probably be avoided for the sake of harmony and peace in the classroom.
2. Students with lower proficiency levels can also take part in opinion gap activities. They just do not have to produce higher levels of language.

References and Further Reading

Brown, H. D. (1994). *Teaching by principles*. Englewood Cliffs, NJ: Prentice Hall Regents.

Clark, J. (1987). *Curriculum renewal in school foreign language learning*. Oxford: Oxford University Press.

Harmer, J. (1983). *The practice of English language teaching*. New York: Longman.

Lee, W. R. (1980). *Language teaching games and contests*. Oxford: Oxford University Press.

Maley, A. (1981). Games and problem solving. In K. Johnson & K. Morrow (Eds.), *Communication in the classroom*. New York: Longman.

Nunan, D. (1989). *Designing tasks for the communicative classroom*. New York: Cambridge University Press.

Prabhu, N. (1987). *Second language pedagogy: A perspective*. Oxford: Oxford University Press.

Wright, A., Buckby, M., & Betteridge, D. (1979). *Games for language learning*. New York: Cambridge University Press.

Appendix: Sample Pop Quiz

1. Percentage of Super Bowl viewers who do not live in the United States
   a. 11   c. 64
   b. 27   d. 89

2. Average length of a professional football player's career, in years
   a. 3.2   c. 6.8
   b. 5.1   d. 8.2

3. Rank of drunk driving among the most common reasons an American is arrested
   a. 1   c. 3
   b. 2   d. 4

4. Rank of the United States among all countries in arms sales to Somalia since 1985
   a. 1   c. 5
   b. 3   d. 7

5. Percentage of Jewish settlers on the West Bank who consider themselves "religious"
   a. 8   c. 48
   b. 28   d. 82

6. Price of a box of Cheerios in Japan
   a. $1.20   c. $5.20
   b. $3.20   d. $7.20

Contributor

Mehmet Ali Cicekdag is a faculty development specialist at the Defense Language Institute in Monterey, in California, in the United States.

◆ Pronunciation
Pronunciation:
Syl/la/bles and Linking

Levels
Beginning-low
intermediate;
particularly for learners
whose L1 is not stress
timed

Aims
Identify syllables
Link words

Class Time
30 minutes

Preparation Time
15 minutes

Resources
Tape player and
audiotape (optional)
Handout with one
paragraph of a short
story that could be
continued by students
or that you will add to
later
Blank audiotape for
each student (optional)

Learners often have difficulty with the rhythm of English, particularly if their L1 is syllable timed. To help overcome this problem, the following activity involves the students actively in learning syllables and linking words in a stream of speech. This activity can be extended to include any part of the sound system that is being taught.

Procedure

Session 1

1. Introduce the counting of syllables by having students tap on their desk with their hand for each syllable of the word that you say. Then put the students in small groups and have them bounce up and down in their seats or clap, while counting aloud the syllables in each word.
2. Prepare a handout of the first paragraph of a story, real or invented.
3. Play the tape or read the paragraph a couple of times, having the students follow along with their handout.
4. In pairs, have the students mark and number each syllable in each word in their handout, and then practice pronouncing the words.

Session 2

1. Decide which sound(s) the students will learn to link, based on the paragraph of the previous week (e.g., the /r/ sound in *hear us* and the stop sound /d/ to the vowel that follows it, as in *told us*).
2. Put the students in pairs.
3. At random, call out two-word patterns in a conversational style that can be linked, intermixed with two-word patterns that are not linked

(e.g., *they plan, there_ is, might go, pair_ of*). These patterns can be increased to phrases.

4. Tell the students to link arms if they hear the correct pattern. Students are out of the game if they link incorrectly.
5. Refer the students to their handout of the previous week.
6. Play the tape or read the paragraph a couple of times with the students following along. Have the students use a linking symbol (e.g., _) to mark their text. Ask the students to practice the linked phrases in pairs or groups.

Caveats and Options

1. This idea can be carried over to other parts of the sound system that need to be practiced, with the added option of having the students continue the story in their own words. Doing this in groups works well. It is easier for the teacher to monitor a group and to check that every student is practicing and marking the relevant sound.
2. Have students change groups to read or role-play their story.
3. Have the students record their story.
4. By the end of a semester, students should be very familiar with their short story, which can be very useful for subsequent student evaluation.

Contributor

Valerie A. Benson is a professor at Suzugamine Women's College in Hiroshima, in Japan. Her research interests include pronunciation and teaching with video.

Stress Clapping

Levels
Beginning–intermediate

Aims
Identify intonational
stress at the sentence
level

Class Time
15 minutes

Preparation Time
None

Resources
Overhead projector
(OHP), overhead
transparencies (OHTs),
and a marker
Extracts from poems,
limericks, and song
lyrics

Students, particularly students whose L1 is a syllable-timed language, may have problems identifying and producing stressed words at the sentence level and above. This game gives students the chance to focus on intonational stress in the informal setting of a game.

Procedure

1. Write sentences or pairs of sentences taken from song lyrics, poems, or limericks. These should be written on OHTs with a marker and cut into strips. Put these folded strips of transparency into a box.
2. Have students form groups of five. Ask a student from one of the groups to come to the front of the class and pull out one of the strips.
3. Put the transparency strip on the OHP and project it.
4. The student must read the sentence or sentences aloud and clap each time there is a stressed word. The student receives a point for each stressed word correctly identified.
5. The group that has accumulated the greatest number of points for correctly identifying stressed words wins.

Caveats and Options

1. Karaoke books of English songs and collections of modern English poetry for young people are good sources of material for this game.
2. The complete song lyrics or poem can be presented to the class as a follow-up to the game.
3. A recording of the song can be played to the students. The students listen and mark the stressed words on a lyric sheet.

4. Students write their own sentences from songs or poems they may know. These are then used for the game.

Contributor

Dino Mahoney is an associate professor in the English Department of the City University of Hong Kong. He also has taught ESL/EFL in England, Greece, and the United Arab Emirates.

What Am I Saying?

Levels
Beginning-intermediate

Aims
Take greater notice of
stress and intonation
patterns and how these
signal meaning in
utterances

Class Time
10-30 minutes

Preparation Time
20 minutes

Resources
Cards with a dialogue or
list of different
utterances

This game enables learners to practice stress and intonation and to use them to signal and identify meaning.

Procedure

1. Give cards to all the learners, organizing them into pairs A and B.
2. Explain the procedure and demonstrate with one or two students.
3. In pairs, A mimics the stress and intonation of the dialogue or utterance on the card using a repeated nonsense word like *N.H.* Listening to the pattern, B tries to identify the sentence that A mimicked.
4. Students may take turns mimicking utterances and identifying them. They may score points for the utterances they correctly identify.

Caveats and Options

1. The complexity of the utterances used will depend on the level of the students and the particular pronunciation focus you have in mind.
2. This activity may be too challenging for students with little experience in hearing spoken English. You could model the utterances first with the whole class and, if necessary, ask the students to repeat after you. When you feel the class has a reasonable grasp of the stress and intonation required, you can start the main stage of the activity.
3. You may wish to do some follow-up work to this game and have students identify the likely stress and intonation patterns for particular utterances.
4. Using a suitable notation system, you could ask students to mark the stress and intonation contours of the utterances before they start

speaking. Alternatively, this could be done as a follow-up exercise to heighten awareness of the patterns employed.

References and Further Reading

Ladefoged, P. (1993). *A course in phonetics*. Fort Worth, TX: Harcourt Brace.

Maley, A., & Duff, A. (1982). *Drama techniques in language learning*. Cambridge: Cambridge University Press.

Scher, A., & Verrall, C. (1987). *Another 100+ ideas for drama*. London: Heinemann Educational Books.

Appendix: Sample Utterances

Excuse me. Can I help you?
Excuse me. This is my seat.
Excuse me. What time does the train leave for Tokyo?
Could you pass the salt?
Is that for here or to go?
I come from China but I was brought up here in Los Angeles.
Actually, I did call you but you were out.
I'd like to book a room for October 3, 4, and 5.
It was great. I just lay on the beach for 10 days.

Contributor

Dominic Cogan is a lecturer at Fukui Prefectural University, in Japan.

That Sounds Right

Levels
High intermediate +

Aims
Practice pronunciation
from phonetic symbols
found in dictionaries

Class Time
20 minutes

Preparation Time
30 minutes

Resources
Flashcards or overhead
transparencies (OHTs)
and an overhead
projector (OHP)

This game gives advanced learners a chance to consolidate their basic knowledge of phonetic symbols. It focuses on the learners' ability to recognize the symbols and provides opportunities for them to pronounce words accurately.

Procedure

1. Choose approximately 50 words, both long and short, from the students' course book. Include another 10 nonsense words.
2. Write each word in phonetic symbols on individual flashcards. Alternatively, if an OHP is available, list them on OHTs. Do not write more than eight words on each OHT.
3. Divide the class into two or three groups, depending on the size of the class. Preferably there should be no more than 10 people in each group.
4. Appoint a timekeeper who doubles as recorder of scores.
5. Explain the rules to the class.
6. Flash in front of a student one of the strings of phonetic symbols that may or may not make up a real word.
7. Give the student who is answering 15 seconds to decide whether the symbols represent an English word. The student should answer only once by saying yes or no. If the word is an English word and the student answers correctly, give the group 1 point.
8. Next, ask the student to pronounce the word. Give 1 point for a word pronounced correctly. If it is a nonsense word and the student pronounces it correctly, give the group 2 points.
9. Repeat the same process with a student from another group and so on.
10. At the end of the game, add up the scores and declare the winner.

Caveats and Options

1. To make the task more challenging, choose only polysyllabic words and award points only when words are said with the correct stress.
2. To add variety to this game, you could include phonetic transcriptions of all of the students' names. This could be introduced as a different round. Because most of these names will probably not be English names, you could omit the stipulation that students say the words with correct stress. They would simply say aloud the name from the transcription.
3. Once students are familiar with the requirements of this game, have them work in groups and produce their own list of words. They can then challenge the other groups with these words.
4. This game is more suitable for small classes.

Contributors

Christine C. M. Goh and Cheah Yin Mee are lecturers in the School of Arts, National Institute of Education, Nanyang Technological University, in Singapore. Goh is interested in the teaching of oral communication skills for general and academic purposes. Cheah's interests are in language and literacy education at the primary school level.

A Sound Match

Levels
High intermediate +

Aims
Practice pronunciation
from phonetic symbols
found in dictionaries
Provide opportunities to
ask questions orally

Class Time
20 minutes

Preparation Time
30 minutes

Resources
Pieces of paper with
words written in
orthography and
phonetics

This game gives learners a chance to review phonetic symbols introduced formally in earlier lessons. They must look for people who have slips with an orthographic or phonetic version of the words they have. This game also encourages oral interaction in that learners have to move around and ask one another questions.

Procedure

1. Select words that your students have learned and copy them in pairs, first in orthographic and then in phonetic symbols. Have at least two pairs of words for every student in the class.
2. Next, copy each version of the words on a small card. You will need two sets of different-colored cards. On one set, write the words in orthography, and on the other set, write the words in phonetics. Put the different-colored cards in two separate boxes.
3. In class, pass the boxes around. Tell each student to pick two cards from each of the boxes.
4. As soon as everyone has received the cards, have students get up from their seats and search for the people with a different version (orthographic or phonetic) of the words they have.
5. When they have found someone with a match, have them come back to you in pairs. If the two words match, award a point to each person. (Devise your own system of keeping score.)
6. The first person to find a match for all of his or her words or score 4 points is the winner.
7. Continue until all of the students have found their matches. (You might want to set a time limit for this.)

Caveats and Options

1. Some students may get an unfair advantage if their words have initial consonants that are easily recognizable, such as /b/, /d/, or /m/. To avoid this, choose words with less straightforward symbols, such as /dʒ/ or /θ/, or words that begin with a common consonant.
2. To utilize the resources more fully, collect all the cards from the participants and go through each word in phonetics with the whole class.
3. You can reduce teacher preparation time by asking each student to produce two pairs of words. Put these in two separate boxes, one for each spelling, and redistribute them. The advantage of this is that learners get more practice with phonetics.
4. Be prepared to put up with some noise.

Contributors

Christine C. M. Goh and Cheah Yin Mee are lecturers in the School of Arts, National Institute of Education, Nanyang Technological University, in Singapore. Goh is interested in the teaching of oral communication skills for general and academic purposes. Cheah's interests are in language and literacy education at the primary school level.

Part II: Learning Content Matter

Editors' Note

The activities in this section use materials that focus learners' attention on ideas and encourage the processing of the subject matter. They help students develop language skills within a content area. Generally, the content area is one that students are already familiar with or will need to be upon the completion of study. The activities are particularly useful for classes with immigrant and minority-group students for whom access to and use of available knowledge is as important as their language abilities, if not more. The activities allow students to practice language skills within a useful, authentic, and specific content area and can be used to teach and practice language skills across the curriculum.

The section concentrates on learning and practicing four language skills: vocabulary, reading, writing, and speaking, in specific content areas. Listening is a latent aim in almost all communicative activities involving speaking, and is therefore included in many of the activities in this section.

◆ Guessing Words in Context
The Attribute Game

Levels
Any

Aims
Practice matching
various attribute names
(e.g., number, color,
shape, size) with the
appropriate picture and
print symbols

Class Time
20 minutes

Preparation Time
1 hour

Resources
Set of reusable picture
cards

You can select the target learning items in this game from any topic or content area. It is easy to adjust the complexity of the game to the level of the students simply by adding or removing the number of attributes for practice.

Procedure

1. Prepare sets of cards (four to six for each student) with pictures of the target language items. If the students are upper primary, secondary, or adult students, you may ask them to make the cards themselves as a preliminary practice activity. In this case, they may draw the pictures or cut them out of magazines that you supply.
2. Organize the students into groups of four to six. Give each group a set of cards. Demonstrate the game with one student or group of students.
3. Each student must ask another player for a card with a certain attribute, such as shape (see Appendix).
4. If the student asks for a card that another player has, the player with the card must place it face up on the table so the other group members can verify that the question was asked and answered correctly before the student can add the card to his set.
5. In a clockwise direction, students take turns asking each other for cards. The student who gets the highest number of cards is the winner.

Caveats and Options

1. At the low intermediate level, only one attribute should be practiced, such as color. However, as students become more proficient, or for students at more advanced levels, combinations of attributes (e.g., color and size) can be introduced.

2. The game may also be played with pictures of objects from other relevant semantic or topical areas (e.g., transportation, clothing, fruit, vegetables, furniture, clothing, animals).

Appendix: Sample Dialogues

Low Intermediate Level (One attribute: shape)

Student A: *Do you have a square?*
Student B: *Here you are* [or *No, sorry, I don't.*]

Advanced Level (Four attributes: number, size, color, shape)

Student A: *Do you have four large, red circles?* [or *Can I have six small, green triangles?*]
Student B: *Yes I do* or [*Sorry, I only have blue ones.*]

Contributor

Carol MacLennan is a senior lecturer at the Hong Kong Institute of Education.

The Supermarket Treasure Hunt

Levels
Any

Aims
Learn supermarket-
related vocabulary
Practice spoken English

Class Time
1 hour

Preparation Time
1 hour

Resources
Work sheets

In this game, pairs or groups of students work together in teams to find the necessary information to complete a treasure hunt. Using prepared work sheets, students hunt for information or items inside a supermarket. Most of this information can be obtained from the product labels or display counters; however, in some instances, students will need to ask questions of store employees (e.g., deli counter workers, cashiers). The winner of the treasure hunt is the first team to complete its work sheet correctly and return to the finish line.

Procedure

1. Take students to the supermarket and distribute work sheets at a spot designated as the start and finish line.
2. Put students into teams of two or three.
3. Inform students that the first team to complete its work sheet correctly and return to the finish line is the winner. To make the game more challenging, set a time limit for completing the work sheet, usually 30–60 minutes. Also establish a penalty for wrong answers and a reward for the winners.
4. Signal the start of the game and ask students to explore the supermarket in search of the information or items requested on the work sheet (see Appendix).
5. Once the teams have completed the treasure hunt and returned to the finish line, check their work sheets for accuracy and announce the winners.

Caveats and Options

1. Review necessary vocabulary beforehand. The treasure hunt could be part of a unit on shopping for food.
2. The start and finish line can be inside or outside the supermarket.

Appendix: Sample Work Sheet

3. After completing the game, have the students compare their work sheets for accuracy and determine the winners.

Name of students on team

How much does an 8-oz (237-ml) can of chicken noodle soup cost?

List two items in the store for which, if you buy one, you can get a second one free.

How much is cabbage per pound/kilogram?

Name one brand of ice cream found in the freezer section.

What brand of bath soap is on sale this week?

At the meat counter, find out the price of sirloin steak.

Contributor

Phil Plourde teaches at English for Internationals at Vanderbilt University, in Nashville, Tennessee, in the United States. He is interested in computer-assisted language learning and ways of getting students to communicate in English in interesting and productive ways.

Guess My Combination

Levels
Any

Aims
Learn colors
Express and support
opinions

Class Time
Variable

Preparation Time
10-15 minutes

Resources
Index cards
Markers (8-10 different
colors)
Chalkboard or
whiteboard

This guessing game helps students practice the vocabulary they have acquired and allows them to use their thinking skills. Students become very involved in the game because they are challenged to find a hidden color combination picked by the teacher. Using their analytical skills and logic, students may explain whether or not classmates' guesses are correct.

Procedure

1. Give each student 8-10 index cards.
2. Demonstrating first with your own set of index cards, ask your students to mark each of their cards with a different color. Each student's set of cards should have the same colors.
3. Holding your cards so that your students cannot see the colors, explain to them that you are going to pick a combination of three colors from your set. Do not show them which three you have chosen.
4. Ask your students to guess the three colors you have chosen. Have them refer to their own cards to help them decide. Write their answers on the chalkboard or whiteboard and indicate the number of colors in your combination they have guessed correctly. For example, if your combination is *yellow-green-brown* and your students say *red-purple-white*, write the number 0 next to this combination.
5. Explain that none of those colors is included in your combination and that students should put those cards aside and rule out guessing those colors again.
6. Repeat the process, helping students use their analytical skills to look at the number of correct guesses to determine, through process of elimination, which colors are in your combination.

7. The student who guesses correctly picks a new color scheme and the rest of the class uses the same procedure to guess the combination.

Caveats and Options

1. Beginning-level students only need to know the names of the colors.
2. Intermediate-level students might need to review or practice certain verbs (e.g., *remove, add, take out*), prepositions (e.g., *instead of, besides*), and statements of opinion (e.g., *I think that* or *That is not right*).
3. Advanced-level students may use all the vocabulary that they already know (e.g., "*Perhaps* we should *replace* red with green" or "*Maybe* we should *substitute* yellow for blue").
4. Give students as many chances as necessary at the beginning. When they understand the mechanics of the game, you can make it more challenging by limiting their guesses to seven or by adding more colors to your combination.
5. Later on, you can divide your students into groups of four or five, name one leader, and let them play following the same procedure.
6. Once they have guessed correctly, ask your students to use a dictionary to see if that combination of colors is found in the flag of any country and, if so, to identify the country.

Contributor

Francisco Ramos, MA TESOL, is a bilingual teacher in the Los Angeles Unified School District, in California, in the United States.

Who Did It?

Levels
Beginning

Aims
Remember the names of colors
Remember the names of clothing items

Class Time
10 minutes

Preparation Time
5 minutes

Resources
None

This guessing game allows students to memorize colors and names of clothing items that have been explained in the previous class. They become engaged in the task because they have to pay attention and listen to clues from their teacher or classmates.

Procedure

1. Ask your students to stand and form a line facing you.
2. Explain to them—exaggerating your tone of voice and adding some mystery to it—that there has been a beauty contest or that a student in your class has just won a box of chocolates and others must guess the winner.
3. Give the students clues by describing something the person you have in mind is wearing, such as, "That person is wearing blue pants." Ask the students who are not wearing blue pants to take their seats but to continue playing by listening to the rest of the clues and guessing the person.
4. Start by giving the students five clues, one at a time. The game is over when someone guesses the correct person.

Caveats and Options

1. Once your students have learned to play, you can divide them into two, three, or four groups and choose one person from each group to give the clues.
2. To increase the challenge of the game according to the level of your students, you can add physical attributes to the clues (e.g., age, hair color).

Contributor

Francisco Ramos, MA TESOL, is a bilingual teacher in the Los Angeles Unified School District, in California, in the United States.

Design a Menu

Levels
Beginning

Aims
Review and expand
vocabulary
Practice language
functions

Class Time
15–30 minutes

Preparation Time
5 minutes

Resources
Chalkboard or
whiteboard
Chalk or markers

Students use cues to design a menu and role-play a restaurant scene.

Procedure

1. Write the following menu headings on the board: *Appetizers, Main Courses/Entrées, Side Dishes, Desserts, Beverages* (or ask more advanced students to name these headings and suggest others). To enhance the context of this activity, write the headings so that the board looks like a giant menu.
2. Ask students to give one or two examples of foods or drinks they would expect to find under each heading.
3. Conduct a short role play in a restaurant: Act as the waiter or waitress and ask two students to volunteer to act as customers. Take their orders as they look at the menu on the board.
4. Divide the students into pairs and ask them to design their own menus, complete with restaurant name, house specialties, menus of the day, and prices. Encourage them to ask you for new vocabulary and feel free to introduce specific terms such as *fried* and *baked*.
5. Ask students to role-play by visiting their classmates' restaurants. Have one student in each pair act as a waiter or waitress, taking orders and explaining the menu items, while the other partner goes to another restaurant. After one role play, students can switch roles.
6. Try different follow-up activities, such as a lengthy role play highlighting different language functions or an expansion of the menu on the board.

Caveats and Options

1. Give each student a budget (on a slip of paper) to spend on the meal. The student must find a suitable restaurant, order a meal, and leave an appropriate tip.

2. Have a contest for the friendliest waiter or waitress, best menu design, or most creative cuisine. Focus on effective language functions by eliciting suggestions from the class (e.g., *How would you ask for a menu?*). List responses on the board and put stars next to each suggestion (the more appropriate, the more stars):

> * *Bring me a menu.*
> * *I want a menu.*
> ** *Menu, please.*
> *** *Could I see a menu, please?*

Contributor

Dennis Bricault is the director of ESL Programs and an instructor in Spanish at North Park College, in Chicago, Illinois, in the United States. He has 17 years' teaching and administrative experience in Spain, Hungary, and the United States.

Dior or Levis? Shirt or Skirt?

Levels
Beginning-intermediate

Aims
Learn and practice specific vocabulary in a communicative activity

Class Time
1 hour +

Preparation Time
1 hour

Resources
Fashion magazines
Drawing paper

ESL students often find their ability to express themselves limited by vocabulary. For instance, they cannot think of specific words to describe clothes, flowers, and animals. Therefore, it is especially necessary to teach and practice particular groups of words. In this activity students are introduced to vocabulary for different clothing items (e.g., denim jeans, baggy jumper, pleated skirt). They then practice their new vocabulary by designing clothes and presenting their drawings to the class.

Procedure

1. Collect pictures from fashion magazines. Use these pictures to introduce the names of the clothing items.
2. Divide students into pairs. Give each student a piece of drawing paper and have them design an item of clothing for their partner.
3. Ask the students to present their drawings to the whole class.

Caveats and Options

1. This game can be further developed to allow students to practice expressions of likes, dislikes, and preferences, such as:

   I like/enjoy ...
   I dislike/hate ...
   I'm (not) very into ...
   I prefer ... to ...
   I'd rather ... than ...

2. The partner may be invited to explain what she likes or dislikes about the design.

3. Students who are reluctant to draw can be encouraged to trace their picture from a magazine photo and then alter the color or other details of the design.

References and Further Reading

Soars, J., & Soars, L. (1990). A sense of taste. *Headway, student's book*. Oxford: Oxford University Press.

Contributor

Eunice Tang is a lecturer in the English Department at the City University of Hong Kong.

Designing a Word Search Puzzle

Levels
Intermediate

Aims
Study vocabulary in context
Scan for specific information

Class Time
30–45 minutes

Preparation Time
15 minutes

Resources
Lexicon dictionary with picture illustrations
Work sheets for students to design crossword puzzles

Vocabulary acquisition can be facilitated if new words are presented in meaningful contexts and with visual aids, such as pictures and authentic materials. The lexicon dictionary is a vocabulary reference book that compares words with related meanings, using examples and illustrations. Students designing word search puzzles with the lexicon are actively involved in learning and are more aware of the correct spelling and meaning of words.

Procedure

1. Photocopy several pages from the lexicon dictionary on chosen topics (e.g., musical instruments, farms, flowers, tools). Sets of words with illustrations or pictures are preferable so that students can see the similarities and differences between words.
2. Design a blank word search puzzle work sheet (see Appendix) with an informative heading at the top (e.g., musical instruments, electrical appliances).
3. Divide the class into groups. Distribute a different lexicon page and work sheet to each group. Ask students to select 10 words they would like to include in the puzzle.
4. Give students 15–20 minutes to design the puzzle by arranging the words in any position—vertically, horizontally, diagonally, and reverse—and randomly filling up the empty spaces with any letters of the alphabet. Explain that the words may overlap where they have a letter in common. For example, *wheel* and *pedal* may overlap at the letter *e* or *l*.
5. When the students have completed designing their puzzles, have the groups exchange only their work sheets. Start the word search game. Explain that the students must identify the 10 words hidden in their puzzles by circling them. The group that finds all 10 words first wins

the game. Have the students return their completed puzzles to the original groups to verify the correct answers.

Caveats and Options

1. This game was designed to increase intermediate-level students' vocabulary and improve their understanding of words that they already know. To adjust the activity for students at a low intermediate level, you may consider allowing students to use the lexicon pages to help them find the hidden words.
2. You can also use this game for vocabulary review by preparing a list of words students have just learned—preferably 10—and asking them to design a word search puzzle.

References and Further Reading

McArthur, T. (1982). *Longman lexicon of contemporary English*. Hong Kong: Longman.

Appendix: Sample Work Sheet

Parts of a Bicycle

In the squares below, design a word search puzzle. Choose 10 words from the information sheet. Arrange the words in any direction: vertically, horizontally, diagonally, or reverse. Words may overlap where they have a common letter. Randomly fill up the empty spaces with any letters of the alphabet.

Information Sheet

wheel	gears
handlebar	derailleur
saddle	frame
pedal	sprocket
chain	fork
brake	kickstand
strap	grip

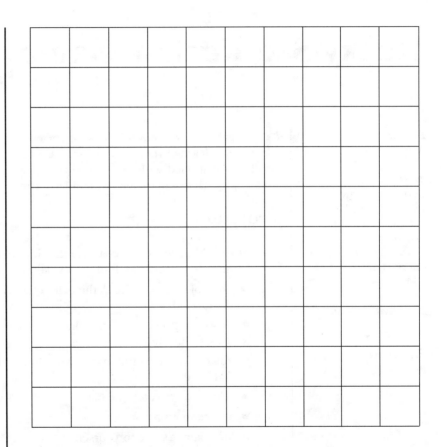

Word Search Puzzle

In this word search puzzle, there are 10 words connected with bicycles. Can you find them?

Remember, you can find the words by reading in any direction: vertically, horizontally, diagonally, and reverse. Circle the words you find.

Contributor

Pauline Tam is a lecturer in the English Department at the City University of Hong Kong.

Hacky-Sac Review Game

Levels
Any

Aims
Review and activate
recently learned
vocabulary and other
material

Class Time
15 minutes

Preparation Time
None

Resources
Hacky-sac

This game is an enjoyable way of reviewing and practicing new and recently learned vocabulary as well as other material. A *hacky-sac* is a small, soft ball filled with beads or rice. It is sold in sports shops. People usually play hacky-sac to keep fit and have fun.

Procedure

1. Move tables, desks, and chairs to the sides of the room. Have students form a circle facing each other. Explain the following rules:

   - The objective is to keep the ball in the air without letting it touch the ground.
   - You cannot use your arms, hands, or anything below your shoulders, to hit the ball.
   - You can use any other part of your body—for example, feet, knees, and head.
   - You may not catch the ball.
   - You cannot say *sorry*.
   - You cannot serve to yourself.
   - If you drop or miss the ball or accidentally kick it out of the circle, your penalty is to think of a word from this week's lesson or topic and give its meaning. Words cannot be repeated.

Caveats and Options

1. This activity is an excellent warm-up and friendship-building exercise.

2. Rather than using this game to review vocabulary, write the words, grammar points, or phrases on the chalkboard or whiteboard. The

penalty would then be to spontaneously construct a sentence using the information provided.

Contributor

Graeme Smith is teaching in Auckland, New Zealand, and has just completed an MA in language teaching at the University of Auckland.

Test Your Concentration

Levels
Intermediate +

Aims
Practice known
functions in a
communicative situation
Practice descriptive
vocabulary

Class Time
30 minutes

Preparation Time
1 hour

Resources
Chalkboard, whiteboard,
or index cards
Chalk, pens

This game encourages students to expand their vocabulary knowledge by learning items from each other within a given thematic area.

Procedure

1. Divide students into groups of three.
2. Explain that the objective of the activity is to practice new vocabulary in real-speech situations and remind them of the theme (e.g., personal appearance).
3. Tell students a story about a robbery.
4. Ask the students in each group to role-play the characters involved in the crime: victim, eyewitness, and police officer. Direct the victims and eyewitnesses to give their accounts of the crime to the officers on duty, describing in detail what happened and what they saw. Encourage the characters to act out the events. Allow the police officers to then ask questions.
5. Because the objective of the role play is to use as many vocabulary words as possible, students who use the most vocabulary words to describe their attacker may be declared the winners of the game.
6. Supply students with the minimum list of vocabulary words and phrases to use in their reports and queries (see Appendix).
7. Walk around the classroom, listening to students and writing down difficulties and mistakes in language production. These can be analyzed together in class after the activity is over.
8. Have students swap roles for further practice.

Caveats and Options

1. You can tailor the vocabulary list to the vocabulary covered on the theme and students' proficiency level in English.

References and Further Reading

Finocchiaro, M., & Brumfit, C. (1983). *The functional-notional approach.* Oxford: Oxford University Press.

Rivers, M. W. (1983). *Speaking in many tongues.* Cambridge: Cambridge University Press.

Appendix: Sample Vocabulary List on Theme of Personal Appearance

Hair: *blond, auburn, black, close-cut, banged, bald, short, long*

Head: *big, small, square, oval*

Face: *chubby, clean-shaven, stubbly, dimpled, hollow, sunken, mustached, bearded*

Build, figure, and bearing: *tall, short, solid, powerful, heavy, strong, delicate, broad, slender*

Manners: *awkward, bashful, clumsy, self-confident, cocky, aggressive, hateful, engaging, sweet, charming, cunning*

Voice: *clear, deep, high-pitched, hoarse, loud, low, shrill, pleasant*

General appraisal of a person's appearance: *air, face, hands, possible age, clothing*

Contributor

Alexander Astor is an assistant professor in the English Department of Hostos Community College, City University of New York, in the United States.

◆ Developing Reading Skills
Classified Ads

Levels
Beginning

Aims
Scan classified ads and
gather information

Class Time
10-20 minutes

Preparation Time
30-60 minutes

Resources
Classified
advertisements from a
local newspaper
Index cards
Copies of information
transfer sheet

In this information search game, students use copies of advertisements to talk to car owners before buying a used car.

Procedure

Before Class

1. Cut out 10-20 classified advertisements dealing with one item (e.g., used cars). Select advertisements with large, clear print and plenty of numbers. Mount each ad on an index card.
2. Develop an information transfer sheet (see Appendix). Include questions and language functions relevant to your students' ability.

In Class

1. Divide the class in half. Distribute an advertisement card to one group (on one side of the room) and an information sheet to the other.
2. Tell the groups their respective roles: The owners have a card and the buyers have an information sheet. Ask students to study their cards and sheets briefly.
3. As a warm-up, elicit language forms that students would expect to use when talking about buying and selling a car. If desired, write selected forms on the chalkboard or whiteboard.
4. Tell the buyers to select two or three cars they would be most interested in buying and find the owners of those cars.
5. Once the buyers and sellers have met, tell the buyers to write down the necessary information about the cars on the sheet. The pairs should discuss the car's features and agree to the terms of the sale. If the buyers are not satisfied, they may move on to another seller.
6. After a few minutes, try a wrap-up role play and discuss appropriate questions and answers and the use of numbers.

Caveats and Options

1. This activity works well with a unit on large numbers, shopping, or likes and dislikes.
2. Instead of cars, you could substitute apartments, houses, electronics, or appliances, to name a few.
3. If you wish to focus on information not included in all of the advertisements, write the data on the card below the advertisement. For example, I included mileage on each card, using a different large number for each advertisement.

Appendix: Sample Information Transfer Sheet

Buying a Used Car

Choose two cars from the list below. Then find the owner and talk about the car (see the sample questions below). Write the price and mileage and decide whether you want to buy the car. If not, keep looking!

Do you have a 1984 Buick Century Wagon?
How much does it cost?
How many miles does it have on it?

	PRICE	MILEAGE
Buick Century Wagon, 1984	_____	_____
Chevy Cavalier, 1984	_____	_____
Pontiac Sunbird, 1984	_____	_____
Chevy Celebrity, 1985	_____	_____
Chevy Cavalier, 1985	_____	_____
Mercury Cougar, 1985	_____	_____
Chevy Cavalier, 1987	_____	_____
C-1500 Chevy Pickup, 1987	_____	_____
F-150 Ford Pickup, 1987	_____	_____
Cavalier Wagon, 1990	_____	_____

Contributor

Dennis Bricault is the director of ESL Programs and an instructor in Spanish at North Park College, in Chicago, Illinois, in the United States. His interests include materials development for teaching foreign languages.

Pick the Right Ones

Levels
Beginning

Aims
Practice scanning
Practice language
needed in giving
explanations

Class Time
30-45 minutes

Preparation Time
30 minutes

Resources
Books (and files if
applicable) with
different colors, sizes,
authors, and other
characteristics
Bookshelves in the
classroom or school
library
Written instructions for
the teacher's reference

This activity makes students aware that they can scan reading material to search for information. If well developed, this skill will help students read and research more efficiently. Through this activity, students practice scanning for specific items and giving explanations. The activity may be carried out in a classroom with bookshelves or in a school library during English lessons.

Procedure

1. Divide the students into two groups, Group A and Group B.
2. Prepare two lists of instructions for books to be found on the shelves, with directions such as:
   - Find five yellow books.
   - Find six books whose titles begin with *The*.
   - Find four books whose authors' last names begin with the letter *B*.
3. Give one list to Group A and, without letting Group B know the instructions on the list, ask Group A to quietly scan the shelves to find the books. Give them approximately 5 minutes to complete this task.
4. When Group A has finished scanning the shelves and collecting the items on the list, ask Group B to examine the items and guess the criteria Group A used in scanning. Have the students in Group B explain their rationale with statements such as:

   I think you were looking for yellow books because all of these books are yellow.

   I think you were looking for books written by Brown because three of these four books are written by him, except this one. This one, written by Smith, must have been picked up by mistake.

52

5. Group A tells Group B whether the guesses and explanations are correct. If a guess or explanation is wrong, Group B can have another chance to answer correctly. If they guess incorrectly a second time, Group A has to give the correct answer and explanation behind the scanning.

6. Award points to each group based on the following scheme:
   - Give one point for each item picked correctly.
   - Deduct one point for each item picked incorrectly.
   - Give two points for each correct guess.
   - Deduct two points for each wrong guess.
   - Give three points for every appropriate explanation given.
   - Deduct three points for every inappropriate explanation given.

7. Record each group's points. The group with the highest score at the end of all the rounds wins.

8. Have the groups switch tasks. Give Group B the second list and have them scan the shelves for the items on the list, then let Group A guess the reasons for the selections and explain the rationale behind the scanning.

Caveats and Options

1. Students at a more advanced level may be allowed to ask the scanning group questions after an incorrect guess to obtain hints for the second guess, for example:

   Did your choice have something to do with color?
   Did the author's surname play a role in your choice?

2. If time allows, students may be asked to put the books back onto the shelves following the order of the call numbers. This gives students another chance to practice scanning (for the appropriate call numbers of books on the shelves) and helps them understand library classification systems.

Contributor

Belinda Ho is an assistant professor in the Department of English at City University of Hong Kong. She has taught ESL and EAP and is now teaching ESP.

Desktop Shopping

Levels
Beginning–intermediate

Aims
Skim and scan texts to
locate relevant
information
Select and organize
information for a
specific purpose
Maintain interaction
through responding and
turn-taking
Speak audibly and
fluently

Class Time
1½ hours

Preparation Time
Enough time to prepare
work sheets and select a
catalogue

Resources
Sales catalogue
Work sheet based on
any sales catalogue and
proposed scenario

This enjoyable, communicative activity helps students integrate reading, cognitive, interpersonal, and speaking practice.

Procedure

1. Divide students into pairs or groups and give them each a copy of a sales catalogue (use authentic originals as much as possible).
2. Tell students that they have $300 (or any stipulated amount based on the general cost of items in the sales catalogue) in their savings account and may use that to buy presents for members of their family.
3. Have students pick presents suitable for their family members and state their reasons for choosing those particular items. Make sure they spend within the budget.
4. Give students a work sheet to complete (see Appendix).
5. Ask students to present their choices to smaller groups or to the whole class.

References and Further Reading

Lim, L. C. (1994). Junk mail galore. *Teaching of English Language and Literature, 10* (1).

Lund, S. (1992). Giving your courses a dose of reality. *English Teaching Forum*.

Appendix: Sample Work Sheets

Student Work Sheet

Family Member	Brief Description	Choice of Gift	Reasons for Choice	Cost
Father	Father is 40 years old. He is unemployed. He is interested in sports and gardening.			
Mother	Mother is 36 years old. She is a doctor. She enjoys relaxing at home on weekends.			
Big Sister	Big Sister will soon be going to Australia for further studies. She is outgoing and has many friends.			
Big Brother	Big Brother has just started work. He is active and, like Father, is very interested in sports.			
Total Cost				

Work Sheet With Response

Family Member	Brief Description	Choice of Gift	Reasons for Choice	Cost
Father	Father is 40 years old. He is unemployed. He is interested in sports and gardening.	A yellow T-shirt	A T-shirt is casual. Father will prefer theyellow rather than the red one. He can wear it in the garden.	$25
Mother	Mother is 36 years old. She is a doctor. She enjoys relaxing at home on weekends.	A book	Mother likes to read nonfiction and it is a book she's always wanted.	$20
Big Sister	Big Sister will soon be going to Australia for further studies. She is outgoing and has many friends.	A pair of gloves	They will be useful in the cold weather when she goes out to visit friends.	$10
Big Brother	Big Brother has just started work. He is active and, like Father, is very interested in sports.	A set of playing cards and a pair of socks	He enjoys playing card games, and the socks will be useful for all occasions, at play and at work.	$8
Total Cost				$63

Contributor

Lim Lai Cheng is an English language specialist inspector at the Ministry of Education, in Singapore.

Murder Mystery

Levels
Low intermediate +

Aims
Read for a purpose
Explore the narrative
point of view and how
it influences what is
written

Class Time
45 minutes +

Preparation Time
Variable

Resources
Murder mystery story
written by the teacher
or adapted from another
source
Slips of paper with
character names

Procedure

1. Have students read the murder mystery story several times.
2. Assign each student a different character from the story by randomly distributing slips of paper with characters' names.
3. Ask students to rewrite the story from the point of view of their assigned characters, without revealing their identity.
4. Have students exchange stories and identify the author's character.
5. Tell students that the final objective of the game is to identify who committed the crime. This may be done by selecting students representing all of the characters to read their accounts of the story aloud. The class then discusses the evidence and decides who is guilty.

Caveats and Options

1. This game naturally lends itself to adaptation in terms of the level of difficulty of the text chosen and the number and variety of activities that can be derived from it. At a low intermediate level, it can be used to practice structural elements of the language, such as a change from active to passive voice entailed by different points of view. At a more advanced level, the activity can be used to explore how different types of characters can affect the style of writing.
2. Instead of a murder mystery story, you can use newspaper articles about factual events or issues, such as a story about a local crime or accident, and ask students to rewrite them from their own or a different person's point of view.
3. This activity could be developed further by having students reenact the story from their own perspectives. Alternatively, students can

create and role-play their own Agatha Christie-type mystery scenario, in which some of them, acting as detectives, question their classmates, who are suspected of committing the crime, to establish alibis, motives, and guilt.

References and Further Reading

Ladrousse, G. (1987). *Role play*. Oxford: Oxford University Press.

Maley, A., & Duff, A. (1982). *Drama techniques in language learning*. Cambridge: Cambridge University Press.

Scher, A., & Verrall, C. (1987). *Another 100+ ideas for drama*. London: Heinemann Educational Books.

Steinberg, J. (1991). *Games language people play*. Markham, Canada: Dominie Press.

Contributor

Dominic Cogan is a lecturer at Fukui Prefectural University, in Japan.

◆ Cultivating Writing Skills
Not All Texts Are Equal

Levels
Any

Aims
Use information transfer
for collaborative
summary writing

Class Time
2 hours

Preparation Time
30 minutes

Resources
Selected reading texts
Information transfer
grids

This activity makes use of the information transfer technique in a collaborative way. The activity encourages students to see that not all texts are equal and enables them to synthesize information from different texts in preparation for writing a summary.

Procedure

1. Choose a topic for a summary writing task. Design a set of questions that focus on important content relating to the topic. Write these in the top row of the information transfer grid. (See the Appendix for a sample.) Distribute copies of the grid to the class.
2. With the class, brainstorm responses to the questions they may be familiar with. Ask students to enter these responses on the grid in the row, *What we know*.
3. Choose a set of three texts that provide useful content for the writing topic. Divide the students into groups of three and assign one text to each student.
4. Ask each student to fill in the row (*Text 1*, *Text 2*, or *Text 3*) on the information transfer grid with content from the assigned text.
5. Ask students to work in groups to fill in the *Summary* row.
6. Ask students to write a summary.

Caveats and Options

1. The level of difficulty of the task can be varied according to the difficulty of the reading text.
2. The number of texts and group members can be varied.
3. Summary writing can be a group task or can be completed individually.

Appendix: Sample Information Transfer Grid

Topic: Frogs

Topic: Frogs	1. What do tadpoles eat?	2. What do frogs eat?	3. Where can frogs live?	4. What eats frogs?	Other interesting facts/figures
What we know	Fish Flies Mosquitoes	Bees Flies Mosquitoes Sea snails	Under the water In the sea In the pond In lakes On a lily pad Under a lily pad	Dragon spider Giraffe Crocodile Shark Fish Eel	If they live in the sun, they can get sunburned. Somtimes they dry out.
Text 1	Small water plants	Insects	In a fish pond		They go down in the mud when the cold comes. Frogs have long tongues. The frog goes up to breathe.
Text 3	Plants and meat Dead fish	Insects Worms Flies Beetles Slugs Snails Wood lice Caterpillars	On plants the pond Grass	Gulls Birds Snakes Rats Foxes Badgers Hedgehogs	Some frogs are poisonous.
Text 3	Plants Pond weed	Worms Snails Slugs	Some live in trees. Some live in damp areas.	Hedgehogs Owls Turtles	Some frogs have spots on them. Some frogs poisonous and are bright and colorful.
Summary	Plants and meat	Insects	Live where it is damp	Birds, snakes, and small animals	Some frogs are spotted. Some are colorful and some are poisonous.

Contributor

Margaret Franken has taught writing skills and pedagogy classes in a wide variety of situations. She is particularly interested in the use of speaking tasks to improve writing. She is a lecturer at Massey University, in New Zealand.

Headlines

Levels
Low intermediate +

Aims
Develop confidence and
conciseness in telling
stories from own
experiences
Have a chance to speak
and listen at own level,
increase knowledge of
peers, and work on
fluency through
repeated tellings

Class Time
30–40 minutes

Preparation Time
2 minutes

Resources
Headline for model
telling
One strip of paper or a
blank sheet of paper per
student
Thick felt-tipped pens
or markers to write bold
headlines

Headlines encourage students to listen to and tell stories from their own experiences. There is a great deal of repetition as students are encouraged to tell everyone their story individually. This also motivates students to perform at a high level because they have a different audience every time. The activity is based on the learners' personal experiences and, therefore, often elicits a great deal of animation and humor when telling their stories.

Procedure

1. Prepare a headline from a recent experience of your own (or that of a friend or family member). Write the headline in newspaper fashion on a strip of paper, large enough to be seen from the back of the room. The headline should grab the attention of the reader and use newspaper conventions. For example:

Appendix: Sample Newspaper Headline

> ### Teacher on the Edge

2. Before class, practice telling the story behind the headline.
3. Display your headline to the class and ask them to speculate as to what they think the story is about. Tell them the story in an entertaining way and see if students guessed the content.
4. Ask students to write a headline from a story of their own and then tell the story to their classmates. The story can be based on a personal experience or that of a friend or family member.
5. Give them about 10 minutes to write the headlines, using the paper and pens you supply.

6. Ask students to stand and display their headlines for others to see and have them move about the room, telling their stories to their classmates, one at a time. Have them repeat their stories as many times as possible within the class period.
7. Have students put a check mark on their paper every time they tell their story.

Caveats and Options

1. Make audiotape recordings of the stories. Let students rehearse several times to achieve their best narrative. Use these recordings to prepare listening work for them or other classes.
2. Compile the stories from the headlines, publishing them as a class newspaper.
3. Have an awards ceremony to vote for the most original, funniest, and strangest story and the most eye-catching headline.

Contributor

Averil Coxhead has taught in Estonia, Romania, Hungary, England, and New Zealand.

Hand on a Hint

Levels
Intermediate +

Aims
Learn cooperatively
Learn communication
and learning strategies

Class Time
30 minutes

Preparation Time
None

Resources
Paper and pencils

Caveats and Options

Contributor

In this activity students suggest ways of solving the language problems of their classmates.

Procedure

1. Have each student prepare a sheet of paper with one of his own language difficulties explained at the top. For example:
   I have difficulty understanding essay questions.
   I have difficulty starting assignments.
   My spelling is terrible.
   I can't follow the TV news.
2. Pass the papers around the class until each student has written one suggestion for everyone else. Ask students to sign their suggestions for later feedback.
3. Have students report to the class a week later on whether the suggestions helped them solve their problems.

1. Ask students to identify a problem they have in a specific area, for example, writing or speaking.

Marilyn Lewis is a senior lecturer at the Institute for Language Teaching and Learning, at the University of Auckland, in New Zealand.

Channel B News

Levels
Intermediate +

Aims
Practice oral
communication skills in
an interactive and
enjoyable context
Practice report writing

Class Time
20 minutes

Preparation Time
None

Resources
Videotape
Camcorder
TV and VCR

Caveats and Options

Contributor

Procedure

1. Assign two students the roles of news reporters.
2. Divide the class in half and assign each news reporter to one of the two groups. Ask the news reporters to interview their classmates outside of class about an important personal experience or event from the previous week.
3. Ask the news reporters to compile the news they gathered in the form of a written report (the format for which you need to decide on and discuss ahead of time).
4. Edit the reports for content and correctness.
5. Videotape the news reporters delivering their reports to the class as if they were professional news anchors.
6. Following the same steps, assign two different students to conduct the interviews and report the news. Ask the class to describe different events each time they are interviewed.
7. Periodically view the videotape for follow-up class discussion about oral communication skills.

1. This game can be an ongoing activity, extended throughout the semester on a weekly, biweekly, or monthly basis.
2. You can name this activity after the class you teach, for example, Channel B News, for a *Level B* class.

Zubeyde Tezel is an EFL teacher and teacher trainer in Turkey. She is currently teaching at the American Language Institute, Indiana University of Pennsylvania, in the United States.

Genre Writing

Levels
Intermediate +

Aims
Write in a particular genre
Use new vocabulary

Class Time
30 minutes +

Preparation Time
5 minutes

Resources
Blank sheet of paper for each student

This activity is an enjoyable way for students to use vocabulary they are learning and to practice writing in a particular genre.

Procedure

1. Choose a particular genre that the students are familiar with (e.g., writing letters to a newspaper). Choose 10 words that students are currently learning on a particular topic and list them on a sheet of paper. Leave enough space between each word for students to write their sentences. Photocopy this sheet so that each student can have a copy.
2. Have the students sit in a circle with their pen, dictionary, and vocabulary notebooks. Explain that they are going to write a series of sentences on a particular topic using a particular style of writing—for example, a letter to the editor giving their opinion on the topic. Have them write one sentence for each word they are given.
3. Give each student a copy of the sheet with the words. Ask the students to write a sentence with the first word on the page and then fold the paper so that their sentence is hidden but the next word on the list is still visible. Tell students that they can consult their dictionaries and vocabulary notebooks, or ask you for help.
4. When students have finished, have them pass their sheets of paper to the student on their right, who writes a sentence with the next word on the list. This continues until all the words have been used in sentences. The papers are then returned to the original students.
5. Each student unravels the paper and reads the sentences aloud to the class. You can comment on the use of words or the style in which they have been written.

Caveats and Options

1. Try writing an odd combination of words to make the activity more humorous.
2. Lower level students could write about any topic, making the activity easier.
3. To make the activity more challenging, do not allow students to use dictionaries.

Contributor

Alison Hamilton-Jenkins has recently completed her MA in applied linguistics at Victoria University of Wellington, in New Zealand.

◆ Establishing Speaking Skills
Headline News

Levels
Beginning

Aims
Study the language used
in newspaper headlines

Class Time
15–30 minutes

Preparation Time
30 minutes

Resources
Newspaper headlines
and corresponding
photographs
Index cards
Blank sheets of paper

Newspapers offer ESL/EFL students a rich source of language learning material. In this activity, students match headlines to their corresponding photographs. Study of the language used in headlines can make this powerful means of communication more accessible to students.

Procedure

1. Cut out interesting headlines and their corresponding photographs from newspapers. Cut the headlines in half, making sure not to split word phrases. Paste the beginnings and ends of the headlines onto index cards and the pictures onto blank sheets of paper.

2. Divide the class into three groups and distribute the materials as follows:
   - Group A = Photographs
   - Group B = Beginning of the headlines
   - Group C = End of the headlines

3. Have students walk around the room, asking each other questions to find the missing part of their headlines and the matching photograph (e.g., "What is your headline about? Are there any people in your photograph?"). Instruct them not to show their material to their classmates until they are certain they have located their partners.

4. The first group to identify its members correctly wins the game.

Caveats and Options

1. When all the headlines and photographs have been matched, the triads sit together and display their material. Each triad reads their headline aloud to the rest of the class and explains which clues led them to a match.

Contributor

2. You can make this activity more challenging by including distractors or using more difficult materials.

Geraldine Hetherton is an EFL lecturer at Fukui Prefectural University, in Japan, and has also taught in Europe, Africa, and the Middle East.

Good Riddance

Levels
Beginning

Aims
Use classification and the process of elimination to reinforce vocabulary
Practice yes/no questions

Class Time
30 minutes

Preparation Time
5 minutes

Resources
Picture cards (about 50)
Chalkboard or whiteboard and chalk or markers
Small bowl

T his guessing game is a modified version of 20 Questions. It helps students to identify orally and practice vocabulary within a content area.

Procedure

1. Gather a set of about 50 picture cards.
2. Have students write their names on a small piece of paper. Collect the names in a bowl.
3. Divide the class into two teams.
4. Select one picture card and place it face down so that the students cannot see what it is.
5. Draw a student's name from the bowl and have that student ask a yes/no question to determine the picture you have selected. The student may confer with other teammates but may not have someone else ask the question.
6. Answer the student's question by restating it as a yes or no response. Write the question and response on the chalkboard or whiteboard, allowing students to refer to previous guesses throughout the game (see Appendix).
7. Repeat Steps 5 and 6 until someone guesses the picture on the card. Teams score 1 point for a correct guess.
8. Reveal the picture to the class.
9. Continue playing, repeating Steps 4-8, until all the students have had a chance to ask a question.
10. The team with the most points at the end of the period wins.

Caveats and Options

1. By drawing names rather than alternating between teams, the same team has the chance of guessing twice in a row. This prevents the other team from always having the advantage of guessing the solution after their opponents have narrowed it down.

2. Before starting the game, you may want to review the pictures and vocabulary for 5-10 minutes. This will help students formulate their questions so they are not merely guessing the picture without concentrating on the vocabulary.

3. You may want to give students a list of the pictures so they know the choices and can keep track of the remaining possibilities as others are eliminated.

4. Once someone has correctly guessed the picture and you have shown the picture to the class, you may want to review the questions and responses to ensure that everyone understands why that guess is correct. You may also want to write a brief note beside each question and response highlighting specific vocabulary (see Appendix).

5. You may want to allow the student who guesses correctly to perform Steps 4-8 for the next picture. That student could pick a player from the opposing team to act as secretary for Step 6.

References and Further Reading

Nation, I. S. P. (1990). *Teaching and learning vocabulary*. New York: Newbury House.

Thompson, I. (1987). Memory in language learning. In A. Wenden & J. Rubin (Eds.), *Learner strategies in language learning* (pp. 43-56). New York: Prentice-Hall.

Appendix: Sample Game

Below is a sample game illustrating Steps 4-8 of the procedure using pictures of animals the students have studied. This sample focuses only on the question and response aspects.

Picture Cards: bat, beaver, boa constrictor, buffalo, cat, catfish, chicken, chimpanzee, dog, dolphin, eagle, earthworm, flamingo, fly, giraffe, goat, gorilla, grasshopper, grizzly bear, hippopotamus, horse, hyena, ladybug, moose, moth, mouse, octopus, opossum, owl, oyster, parrot, penguin, pig, porcupine, reindeer, seahorse, seal, shark, sheep, spider, tiger, toad, walrus, wasp, whale, wolf, zebra

Key

> Q = student question
> R = teacher or game leader response (see Caveats and Options, No. 5)
> N = note highlighting vocabulary

Q: Does it live on land?	R: Yes, it lives on land.	N: lives on land
Q: Does it swim?	R: No, it doesn't swim.	N: does <u>not</u> swim
Q: Does it fly?	R: No, it doesn't fly.	N: does <u>not</u> fly
Q: Is it a mammal?	R: Yes, it's a mammal.	N: mammal
Q: Does it live in Africa?	R: No, it doesn't live in Africa.	N: <u>not</u> in Africa in Africa.
Q: Is it wild?	R: Yes, it's wild.	N: wild
Q: Does it live underground?	R: No, it doesn't live underground.	N: <u>not</u> underground
Q: Does it live in a tree?	R: No, it doesn't live in a tree?	N: <u>not</u> in a tree
Q: Does it eat meat?	R: No, it doesn't eat meat.	N: <u>no</u> meat
Q: Is it brown?	R: Yes, it's brown.	N: brown
Q: Is it a grizzly bear?[1]		
Q: Is it a deer?[2]		
Q: Is it a buffalo?	R: No, it's not a buffalo.	N: <u>not</u> a buffalo
Q: Is it a moose?	R: Yes, it's a moose.	(Now show the picture of the moose to the class.)

---

[1] Because *grizzly bear* is obviously an incorrect answer, you may want to respond with a question, such as *Doesn't a grizzly bear eat meat?* If the student says *yes*, you might point out the note on the board, <u>*no meat*</u>, and let the student ask another question. If the student answers *no*, you might simply write <u>*not grizzly bear*</u> on the chalkboard or whiteboard and address this issue in a future lesson.

[2] The picture set might not necessarily include all the associated vocabulary students have learned. How you handle guesses like this one will depend on whether you give your students a list of the pictures before the start of the game.

Now that the students can see the moose, you may want to repeat their questions, focusing just on the moose to reaffirm that a moose fits the description (i.e., "Does a moose live on land? Does a moose swim?"), or using the entire set of pictures to demonstrate the process of elimination (i.e., "Does an angelfish live on land?" "Does a bat live on land?")

In either instance, you can use the opportunity to clarify any vocabulary from the questions by miming (e.g., swimming), pointing (e.g., to Africa on a globe), or calling on volunteers (e.g., "What does wild mean?").

Contributor

Paul Lyddon teaches content-based ESL in grades 6-8 at Piedmont Open Middle School in Charlotte, North Carolina, in the United States.

Invitations Galore

Levels
Beginning-intermediate

Aims
Practice making,
accepting, and refusing
invitations

Class Time
45-60 minutes

Preparation Time
1 hour

Resources
Teacher-made board
game and invitation
cards for every four to
eight students
Die for each board game
Place marker, such as
coins, for each student

This game provides concentrated practice in making and responding to invitations. The students enjoy talking about the things they like to do, and the repetition encourages fluency.

Procedure

1. Have students form groups of four to eight. Give each group a board game, set of cards, and die. Give each student a place marker.
2. Explain the rules of the game:
   - Taking turns, students roll the die, move their space markers the number of spaces indicated on the die, and follow the directions written in the square on which they land.
   - If students are instructed to pick a card, they must express the invitation stated on the card to a classmate (see Appendix). The invited student must accept or reject the invitation and, in the case of a rejection, give a reason.
   - The first student to reach the finish point on the game board wins.

Caveats and Options

1. Because the goal of this game is to review the phraseology of invitations, students should already have studied this function of speech.
2. You may specify on the cards whom to invite, such as *the person on your left* or *the person across from you,* or let the students choose whom to invite.
3. You should use familiar places, events, and activities on the cards.

References and Further Reading

Tillitt, B., & Bruder, M. N. (1985). *Speaking naturally*. Cambridge: Cambridge University Press.

Zelman, N. E. (1986). *Conversation inspirations for ESL*. Brattleboro, VT: Pro Lingua.

Appendix: Sample Game Card Statements

Ask a friend to go with you to the movies.

Ask a classmate to meet you after class so that you can study together.

You and some friends are going for a walk after class. Ask another classmate to go with you. You might stop at a café and get ice cream, too.

You and some friends are going on a picnic next Saturday. Ask a classmate to join you.

Ask someone in the class to go out with you on a date.

You see someone sitting alone in the school cafeteria. Ask that person to join you for lunch.

You are going to visit a relative. Ask a classmate to go with you.

You have two tickets to a soccer game. Ask the classmate to your right to go with you.

A new disco opened up in town. Ask the classmate across from you to go with you to see what it's like.

You have an English video at home. Ask a classmate to come over and watch it with you.

Your little brother or sister is acting in a school play next weekend. Ask a classmate to go with you.

Your family has recently moved into a new apartment. Invite your friends over.

Your dog is taking part in a dog show next weekend. Ask a classmate to go with you.

You're going shopping to buy your mother a gift next weekend. Ask a classmate to go with you.

Your parents just returned from a trip and are going to show their videos of the trip. Ask a classmate to come see them.

You are invited to a party and can bring a friend. Ask a classmate to come with you.

There's an interesting exhibit at the museum. Ask your classmate to go see it with you.

Your best friend is getting married and you are having a party. Ask a classmate who also knows your friend to come to the party.

Your favorite singer is giving a concert and you have two tickets to the performance. Ask a classmate to go with you.

Contributor

Margo Menconi teaches English in Bratsk, Russia.

A Few of My Favorite Things

Levels
Beginning-intermediate

Aims
Ask for personal
information
Practice question tags
for the purpose of
checking information
Get to know classmates

Class Time
30 minutes

Preparation Time
10 minutes

Resources
Sets of four different
question cards for each
group

Students must ask for personal information and use question tags to check the information they receive. The game covers work on intonation and appropriateness within a content area and is a good icebreaker for a first or second class, when students are still getting to know each other.

Procedure

1. Divide students into groups of four. Distribute a different set of question cards to each group so that each student gets one card.
2. For the first task, have students take turns asking the questions on their cards to each member of the group. If there are four questions on a card, students must ask four rounds of questions.
3. Students must elicit personal information and remember it without writing the information.
4. Review the syntax of question tags with the class to show how the speaker checks information with the listener (e.g., *Your favorite city is Kyoto, isn't it? Your favorite food is chicken, isn't it?*). Draw attention to intonation in question tags.
5. For the second task, ask students in the same groups to check their recall of personal information by stating the relevant information followed by a question tag. Follow the same order as in the first task (e.g., *Your favorite color is green, isn't it? Your favorite color is red, isn't it?*). Listeners respond with *Yes, it is* or *No, it isn't.*

Caveats and Options

1. Question tags are very common among native English speakers. Some second language learners have problems with question tags because of L1 interference—for example, using *is it?* or *isn't it?* for all question tags, even when the dummy auxiliary or modal auxiliary is required.

2. Question cards can vary according to the level of the class so that students can practice a variety of question tags (e.g., *Don't you? Weren't you? Isn't he?*).
3. Students may improvise when they cannot recall personal information (e.g., *Tomorrow is a holiday, isn't it?*).

Appendix: Sample Question Cards

Sample Card 1: Beginning
1. What is your favorite food?
2. What is your favorite color?
3. What is your favorite singer's name?
4. What is your lucky number?

Sample Card 2: Intermediate
1. What was your favorite subject at school?
2. Which city is your favorite?
3. Who is your favorite film star?
4. What is the title of your favorite book or magazine?

Contributor

Theresa Thiel is a lecturer on the BEd TESL program in the Faculty of Education, University of Malaya, Kuala Lumpur, in Malaysia.

What's That Fruit?

Levels
Low intermediate +

Aims
Practice communicative
skills and descriptive
vocabulary in a realistic
situation

Class Time
20 minutes +

Preparation Time
None

Resources
Chalkboard or
whiteboard
Chalk or markers

Students are faced with solving a real-life problem by transferring information as accurately as possible, so that considerable monitoring and clarification take place.

Procedure

1. List on the chalkboard or whiteboard fruits familiar to students.
2. Have the students work in pairs. Ask A to tell B, "I bought a fruit from the market today, but I don't know its name." B asks questions about the fruit (e.g., its size, shape, color, texture, smell, flavor, skin; whether it has pits or seeds; what tree or bush it comes from; what season it ripens in; where it grows; and how it is eaten). B guesses the name of the fruit.
3. Ask the students to switch roles.

Caveats and Options

1. Less advanced students can be assisted with written suggestions, such as:

   What size is it? (*Larger than an apple* or *The same size as a watermelon.*)
   Can you eat the skin? (*Yes, but it is sour.*)
   How much are they? (*$2 per bunch.*)
   Does it grow in cold countries? (*No, only in tropical countries.*).

2. This activity can be adapted to other topic areas, such as countries (e.g., *I've just been abroad. Guess where I went?*). Questions can cover size, population, climate, national foods, famous sites, main religions, and local sports.

Contributor

David Hirsh is currently teaching ESL at Assumption University in Bangkok, in Thailand.

How Would You Feel?

Level
Intermediate

Aims
Evaluate a questionnaire
Practice eliciting a
reaction from others

Class Time
30 minutes

Preparation Time
30 minutes

Resources
8–10 *How would you
feel about . . . ?*
questions written on a
handout, overhead
transparency (OHT),
chalkboard, or
whiteboard
One index card per
student

This activity gives students an opportunity to examine a questionnaire and select the questions of special interest to them. The students then conduct a limited questionnaire study among their classmates, paying specific attention to points of agreement and disagreement.

Procedure

1. Display or distribute the questionnaire (see Appendix A).
2. Write the following headings on each index card: Summary Question, Own Reaction, Agree, Disagree (see Appendix B). Distribute one card to each student.
3. Allow the students approximately 5 minutes to study the questionnaire and select three questions that interest them or that they have the strongest reaction to, either positive or negative.
4. Ask students to write a summary of their selected questions, using one word or phrase (e.g., *foreign roommate, different culture, language at work*), and their reaction to each question on their card (e.g., *I would enjoy the experience, I wouldn't like it at all, It makes me uncomfortable*).
5. Divide the class into two groups. One group forms an outer circle (A), and the other group forms an inner circle (B).
6. The circles rotate in opposite directions (i.e., A rotates clockwise and B rotates counterclockwise).
7. At your signal, students in circle A should stop and ask the students facing them in circle B a question from their card.
8. If B strongly agrees or disagrees with A's reaction, then A notes B's name in the appropriate column. If B does not feel strongly, one way or the other, about the question, then A does not note the student's name.

9. A continues to ask B questions until you signal movement by saying, "Rotate."
10. Repeat the procedure, with those in Circle B asking those in Circle A the questions.
11. Repeat Steps 6–9 until all the students have asked each classmate at least one question or until the allotted time has elapsed.
12. Students count the number of classmates who agreed and disagreed with their reactions. The student with the most names may be declared the winner.

Caveats and Options

1. The level of difficulty of this activity can be increased by presenting a topic and requiring the students to devise their own questionnaire.
2. Many topics lend themselves to this game. Topics of special interest to the students or based on reading assignments or project work may be used.

Appendix A: Sample Questionnaire

Topic: Intercultural Experiences

How would you feel about . . .
- having a foreign roommate?
- your sister or brother marrying someone from a different culture?
- living in a foreign country for a year?
- being the only [Japanese/Canadian] in a group?
- using a foreign language at work every day?

Appendix B: Sample Information Card

Summary	Question	Own Reaction	Agree	Disagree
1.				
2.				
3.				

Contributor

Geraldine Hetherton is an EFL lecturer at Fukui Prefectural University, in Japan, and has also taught in Europe, Africa, and the Middle East.

Can You Figure Them Out?

Levels
Intermediate +

Aims
Practice known
language in a
communicative situation
(describing experiences,
asking yes/no questions)
Critically analyze
experiences

Class Time
30 minutes

Preparation Time
None

Resources
None

This is a simple, fast simulation that allows students to experience unanticipated, culturally defined expectations in behavior. Students who play the roles of visitors to a new culture may react with confusion, misunderstanding, and even irritation as they confront unexpected attitudes and behaviors. The end of the exercise can be very revealing and instructive, as students explore how it feels to encounter cultural difference. This exercise is also an excellent review of yes/no questions.

Procedure

1. If you have more than 15 students, divide them into two groups. Make sure the groups contain both males and females. Have the groups sit on opposite sides of the room.
2. Ask for a male and female volunteer from each group to play the role of visitors to a new culture.
3. Take the volunteers outside the classroom and explain to them that they will be visiting an unfamiliar country. Their job is to learn as much as possible about the culture of that country. To do this, they can only ask questions whose answers are yes or no. They should also closely observe the behavior of the members of the culture.
4. Leave the volunteers outside the room and explain to the rest of the class that they should react in the following ways when the visitors question them:
   - Only respond when a visitor of the same sex asks a question. If the visitor is of the opposite sex, look down and do not speak.
   - When answering a question, look at the visitor's facial expression. If the visitor is smiling, answer yes; otherwise, answer no.
5. Call the volunteers back into the room and start the game. Let the questioning continue for approximately 10 minutes.

6. End the activity and have students discuss their reactions. Ask the visitors how they felt about the behavior of the members of the new culture. Encourage learners to explore their feelings and reasons behind them (e.g., I felt out of place when . . . , I felt uncomfortable because . . . , It was quite strange when. . . .).
7. Ask the visitors what they learned about the behavioral expectations or customs of this new culture.
8. Ask members of the new culture how they felt when they were being questioned. Summarize what was learned through this experience.

Caveats and Options

1. Because the final part of this game is extremely important, learners must have at least a minimal level of competence in social interaction with classmates on familiar and unfamiliar topics.

References and Further Reading

Kohls, L. R., & Knight, J. M. (1994). *Developing intercultural awareness: A cross-cultural training handbook.* Yarmouth, ME: Intercultural Press.

Storti, C. (1989). *The art of crossing cultures.* Yarmouth, ME: Intercultural Press.

Storti, C. (1994). *Cross-cultural dialogues: Seventy-four brief encounters with cultural difference.* Yarmouth, ME: Intercultural Press.

Acknowledgment

This activity was suggested by Stella Ting-Toomey (although not as an ESL/EFL exercise) from her Teaching Intercultural Communication course, taught as part of the Summer Institute for Intercultural Communication, Portland, Oregon, July 1995.

Contributor

Clarissa Meléndez, Noemi Rosario, and C. William Schweers have degrees in TESOL and collaboratively teach a course in the English Department of Bayamon Technological University College, in Puerto Rico, where they use innovative lessons to instruct beginning-level EFL students.

The Good Manners Game

Levels
High beginning +

Aims
Become aware of
cultural differences and
norms regarding
common rules of
etiquette
Practice authentic oral
communication

Class Time
1 hour

Preparation Time
2 hours

Resources
Book for each group on
rules of etiquette
One teacher-made board
game with cards for four
to eight students
One die for each group
Place markers such as
coins

This activity offers a relaxed and enjoyable way to discuss social rules of etiquette. Students learn the rules and expectations of another country and are encouraged to compare and discuss related rules of etiquette in their native countries. This activity offers insight into students' sociocultural needs and interests and is, therefore, also an appropriate exercise for a teacher in-service class.

Procedure

1. Divide the students into small enough groups that they can fit around tables.
2. Give each group a game board, set of cards, and die. Give each student a place marker.
   Explain the rules of the game as follows:
   - Students roll the die and move the indicated number of spaces.
   - When students land on a space with instructions, they must follow the directions.
   - If the space indicates a situation or place (see Appendix A), students should say something about etiquette related to that place or situation. This is also a good chance to discuss and compare rules of etiquette in different settings.
   - If the space says *pick a card*, students must pick a card, read aloud the page number indicated on the card, and answer the question on the card (see Appendix B).
   - If the space says *go back* or *go ahead*, students should move the number of spaces indicated.
   - The first person to reach *finish* is the winner.

Caveats and Options

1. The reference book listed below is useful because it covers the basic rules of etiquette that students are most likely to encounter. However, other similar books are also available.
2. If the class is large and there are not enough books to go around, have groups share a book or photocopy relevant pages and distribute them to the groups.

References and Further Reading

Hartley, H. (1990). *The family book of manners.* Westwood, NJ: Barbour.

Appendix A: Place and Situation Spaces

a wedding
in the forest
as a house guest
on the telephone
gift giving
in the store
personal hygiene
in the theatre
at a funeral
in class
at the meal table
on the bus

Appendix B: Sample Questions for Cards

Say something about being a good conversationalist.

What are some rules about hosting a party?

What is *family style*?

How should we chew our food?

What does *regrets only* mean?

Say three things about being seated at the dinner table.

What is one thing considered to be good personal hygiene?

What are some gracious things to say?

What are some rules regarding eating in restaurants?

Say something about listening.

How should we introduce people?

How can we show sports courtesy?

What topics are better avoided in polite conversation?

What are some things you should *not* do on the phone?

How should we answer the phone?

What are some rules about shaking hands?

How should we respond to any gesture of kindness?

Appendix C: Game Board

Below is a copy of the game board.

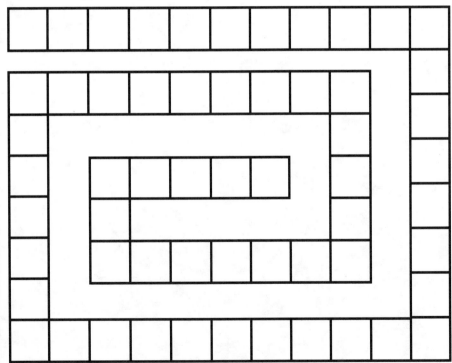

Contributor

Margo Menconi teaches English in Bratsk, Russia.

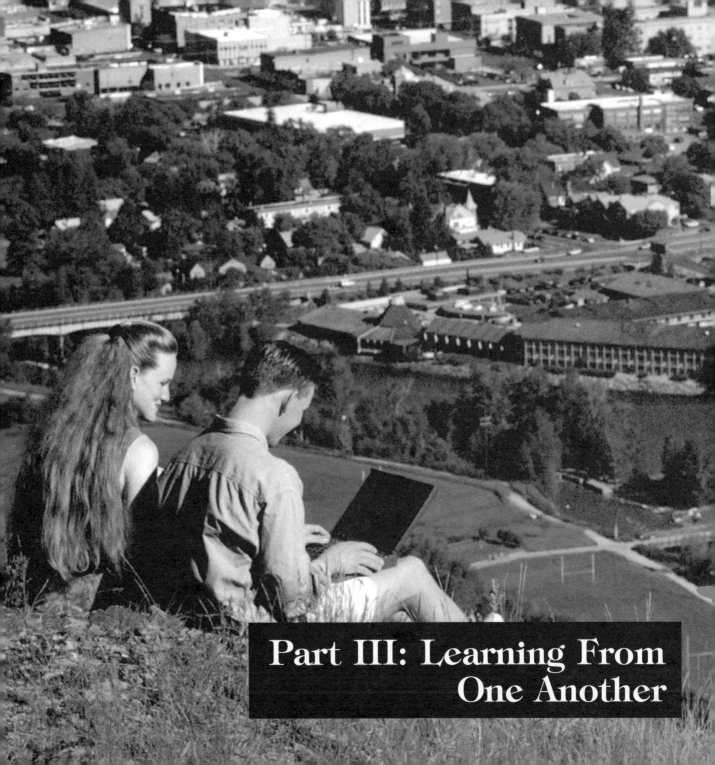

Part III: Learning From One Another

Editors' Note

The rationale for the activities in this section is that students themselves are a powerful learning resource and, working in groups or pairs, can learn language items from each other when the context is nonthreatening. Because the language used is based on context, learners are able to give and request information, negotiate meaning, and make confirmation or clarification requests to check understanding. The activities in this section also encourage students to use language to convey their emotional attitudes to express themselves and consolidate their relationships with other people.

These activities would, therefore, be particularly useful for students who may not have sufficient language skills to understand and respond to the language used outside of the classroom or who tend to use another language to perform similar tasks. It is important to remember, however, that more negotiation occurs when students are less familiar with an activity, so any activity in this section should be used a limited number of times within a class.

◆ Enriching Vocabulary and Productive Use

Audio Stories

Levels
Any

Aims
Practice vocabulary
cooperatively
Engage in spontaneous
conversation
Experience a
communicative context
rich in imagery

Class Time
15-30 minutes

Preparation Time
10-45 minutes

Resources
Audiotape, with sound
sequences 10-30
seconds long

Vocabulary reinforcement does not have to be a mechanical exercise. This game creates opportunities for practicing vocabulary through communicative language use. It promotes cooperative interaction, with students working together in small groups to close an information gap by verbally sharing the feelings and associations that sound sequences awaken in them. The element of the unknown, together with the sound stimulus, animate students' imagination, reduce their anxiety level, and bring a part of the real world into the classroom.

Procedure

1. Select several thematic sound sequences, each 10-30 seconds long, from a commercially available audiotape. Possible sounds include:
   - footsteps, key turning in lock, door opening, footsteps, door shutting, dog barking footsteps running, children shouting, cheering, kicking of ball, crashing of glass
   - buffing of shoes, shoe falling, picking up shoe, brushing off, telephone ringing, footsteps running downstairs, telephone stopping
   - garage door closing, footsteps running, car door opening, car door closing, car starting, car driving off, clapping of thunder, falling of rain
   - opening of cupboard, removal of dishes, fat cooking, egg frying, egg being placed onto a plate and cut with a knife
   - closet door opening, vacuum cleaner starting, vacuuming, stopping, moving of furniture, sweeping, vacuum cleaner being put away

● saw starting, tree being cut, tree creaking, tree falling and crashing to the ground, truck driving off

If such an audiotape is not available, create your own by recording segments with sounds or collating them from other sources. Make sure that the sounds in the segment are thematically or logically connected and depict some type of action so that the sequence will lend itself to building a story.

2. Divide the class into teams of two to four students. Play one sound sequence and allow each team time to guess what the segment is about and arrive at a team consensus.

3. Have a spokesperson from each team present the consensus and the rationale behind it to the rest of the class.

4. Play the sound segment again and tell the class exactly what happens in the story. Have the class decide which team had the most accurate guess, and assign scores (optional) on a scale of 0–3.

5. Repeat Steps 2–4 for the remaining sound sequences. Encourage the teams to appoint a different spokesperson to present their guesses.

Caveats and Options

1. Select sound sequences to target certain desired vocabulary items or topics (e.g., art, sports, cooking, travel, animals, shopping, music).

2. Use the sound story activity as a warm-up for introducing a lesson. After the sound sequence is verified, generate questions leading into the topic of the lesson. For example, you could use the sequence with the vacuum cleaner sounds to introduce the topic of stereotypical male-female roles or the sequence with the saw and falling tree to introduce environmental concerns; the frying egg sequence could lead to a discussion of health issues, eating habits, table manners, or favorite foods. A single sound sequence could be used to introduce a wide variety of topics.

3. Adjust the language and task to the level of the students; for example, have beginning-level students label objects in the sequence with simple phrases, and have advanced-level students use abstract language and discuss hypothetical situations.

4. Present a sound-sequence story and have students in small groups create a follow-up story that continues the situation. Their story could be prepared in written or oral form and presented to the class.

5. Have small groups of students create or select their own sound sequences and bring them to class. Each group of students would then be responsible for running the game and giving feedback to the rest of the class.

Contributor

Grazyna Dudney taught EFL at Wroclaw Polytechnic University in Poland. She is currently a faculty trainer at the Defense Language Institute in Monterey, California, in the United States.

Follow Me

Levels
Beginning

Aims
Listen and repeat
information
Make statements about
self
Practice first- and third-
person singular forms

Class Time
20 minutes

Preparation Time
None

Resources
None

Language games are more interesting and motivational than mechanical drills in helping beginning students acquire grammatical patterns. This game gives students practice in producing simple sentences and helps them learn more about each other. When they enjoy themselves, students feel more relaxed, are apt to talk about themselves, and learn new words in context.

Procedure

1. Ask students to sit in a circle. If the class has more than 20 students, divide them into smaller groups.
2. Ask them to think of a favorite fruit, and then have them take turns introducing their favorite fruit.
3. Ask the next student to repeat the answer of the previous student before introducing her favorite. For example,

    Student 1: I <u>like</u> apples.

    Student 2: Ann <u>likes</u> apples. I <u>like</u> melons.

    Student 3: Ann <u>likes</u> apples. Sam <u>likes</u> melons. I <u>like</u> grapes.

    Student 4: Ann <u>likes</u> apples. Sam <u>likes</u> melons. John <u>likes</u> grapes. I . . . .

    If a student forgets what another has said or makes a mistake, start the game again, with the next student as the first one.
4. Make sure everyone in the group has introduced a favorite fruit. Invite students to repeat the answers. The winner is the one who can remember the most answers correctly.

Caveats and Options

1. This game can be used as an icebreaking activity by asking students to form smaller groups and talk about many other things (e.g., favorite color, cartoon character, pastime, pet, school subject).
2. To make the game easier for a new class, you may distribute sticky labels for students to use as name tags so that they do not need to memorize speakers' names.
3. Some students may need help with vocabulary. Give them a chance to ask questions and provide examples before you start the game.

Contributor

Pauline Tam is a lecturer in the English Department at the City University of Hong Kong.

Animal Psychology

Levels
High beginning +

Aims
Describe self and others
Practice the possessive
Write a creative text
during the
communicative task of
finding a pen pal or a
cyberpal

Class Time
10-25 minutes

Preparation Time
None

Resources
Chalkboard, whiteboard,
or overhead projector
(OHP)
Index cards

In this student-centered activity, students learn to focus on themselves and others. By indirectly describing their favorite animal and sharing their subjective view of why it is their favorite, students become curious about their classmates' choices. Their classmates' rationale for a favorite animal keeps students involved in the task so that they react to classmates' descriptions of favorite animals by acknowledging their observations or challenging their interpretations.

Procedure

1. Pair off students and have them jot on index cards three main characteristics or activities of their favorite animal.
2. Then have partners
   - swap index cards and read one another's three phrases
   - guess the partner's animal and write the name on the back of the partner's index card
   - swap cards again, with each student writing on the front of the index card the name of the animal she had in mind
   - swap cards again and compare
   - present the partner's favorite animal to the class, with the class discussing the animal's qualities, characteristics, and activities
3. Create an activity of association on the chalkboard, whiteboard, or OHP. Write each student's favorite animal and circle it. It is advisable to use no more than eight animal names.
4. Have the class contribute words associated with each animal. Start randomly. The person who mentioned her favorite animal is included in the activity and allowed to respond.

5. Around the circled animal names, jot down key terms mentioned by students. Help with unfamiliar vocabulary and questions in case there is a low student response for a particular animal.
6. Proceed until each pair has mentioned the partner's favorite animal and class contributions to word lists are exhausted.
7. Ask students to pretend they are animal lovers and create a text describing themselves and the partner, penpals, or cyberpals they are looking for. Ask each student to consider some of the characteristics and activities of their favorite animal.

Caveats and Options

1. This warm-up activity presents a prewriting, prediscussion activity. It was designed for students with difficulties in spontaneously expressing themselves in oral and written form. Therefore, you can use the pair and class activities to reactivate vocabulary and to introduce new vocabulary.
2. Students can use a few key phrases, possibly with mime, or tell a short story to describe their partner's favorite animal until classmates guess its name.

References and Further Reading

Angelo, T. A., & Cross, K. P. (1993). *Classroom assessment techniques: A handbook for college teachers*. San Francisco, CA: Jossey-Bass.

Contributor

Claudia Becker teaches intermediate and advanced academic writing classes for international students as well as tests and places students in the English as a Second and International Language Program at Loyola University Chicago. Her research areas include free writing in the initial stages of foreign language acquisition, sociolinguistic aspects of German in the work place, and spoken versus written language proficiency.

Spell It Out

Levels
Beginning–intermediate

Aims
Improve spelling

Class Time
30 minutes

Preparation Time
10 minutes

Resources
Flash cards

Learning to spell is important but can be a burden, especially for speakers of languages with phonetic spelling. This game makes the task enjoyable and collaborative. It also allows the teacher to target particular spelling problem areas.

Procedure

1. Create a set of flash cards. Each card should contain one of a group of words that students are already familiar with (e.g., places, fruit, sports). In each word, blank out the most difficult letters (see the Appendix).
2. Divide the class into three or more teams. Divide the flash cards among the teams.
3. Teams take turns showing each other a flash card for 5 seconds. Each flash card can only be used once. Warn the players that a blank can represent one or more letters.
4. The first team to spell the word correctly gains a point. If a team makes an attempt but fails, other teams can try. The team with the highest number of points after all the flash cards have been used is the winning team.

Caveats and Options

1. Use this game to concentrate on particular pronunciation problems by making different sets of flash cards with words phonetically spelled and vowels, double consonants, or consonant clusters replaced with a blank.
2. Ask teams to make their own flash cards, reducing your preparation time to zero and providing flash cards for use with other classes.

Appendix: Sample Flash Cards

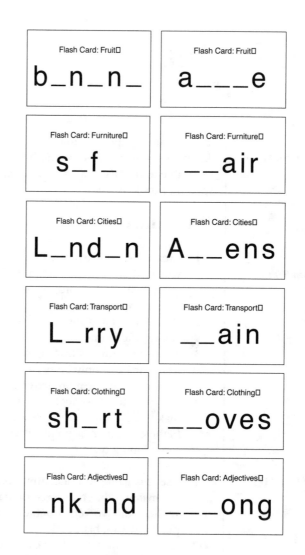

Flash Card: Fruit□

b_n_n_

Flash Card: Fruit□

a___e

Flash Card: Furniture□

s_f_

Flash Card: Furniture□

__air

Flash Card: Cities□

L_nd_n

Flash Card: Cities□

A__ens

Flash Card: Transport□

L_rry

Flash Card: Transport□

__ain

Flash Card: Clothing□

sh_rt

Flash Card: Clothing□

__oves

Flash Card: Adjectives□

_nk_nd

Flash Card: Adjectives□

___ong

Contributors

Lindsay Miller is an assistant professor in the English Department at City University of Hong Kong. David Gardner is a senior instructor in the English Centre at the University of Hong Kong.

Word Market

Levels
Low intermediate +

Aims
Engage in fluency
practice through
student-to-student
negotiation
Learn new vocabulary
Practice spelling
dictation

Class Time
30 minutes

Preparation Time
15–20 minutes

Resources
Pretend money
Work sheet

Caveats and Options

Students compete to make the biggest profit from buying, selling, and exchanging words. Because students see the activity as a vocabulary competition, it provides excellent oral interaction and fluency practice: Even the most cautious students are focused on communication rather than form or correctness.

Procedure

1. Prepare work sheets (see Appendix A) with 15–20 words. Duplicate enough so that every student can have a copy.
2. Ask students to work in pairs. Allow about 5 minutes for them to fill in any words they already know. Ban dictionaries and reference books.
3. Give each student $20 in small notes and explain the objective and rules of the game (see Appendix B).
4. Tell students they can leave their seats and start trading. The first time, you may need to encourage the process by touting words or letters for sale. As soon as students are negotiating with each other, price yourself out of the market.
5. Give a 5-minute warning before you close trading.
6. Close trading and quickly give the correct answers and spellings. Students count up their total assets to see who has won.

1. When choosing words for the work sheet, select words that will occur in another context or will introduce lexical areas or word formation.

2. The ideal difficulty level is when each pair knows a few of the words. Err on the side of difficulty. Students soon realize that any words they buy from you can be sold to their classmates at a profit.

Appendix A: Sample Work Sheet

Jobs	This person:
1. _ _ _ _ _ _ _	looks after your teeth.
2. _ _ _ _ _ _ _ _ _ _	makes and sells medicine.
3. _ _ _ _ _ _ _ _	studies plants.

Appendix B: Objective and Rules

Objective

Students aim to make the most money. At the end of trading, each correct word on the students' paper is worth $5. This sum is added to the amount of cash they have as total assets.

Rules

- No dictionaries or other reference sources may be used.
- Students may buy, sell, or swap words.
- Students may buy words or letters from the teacher.
- There are no fixed prices. All deals are negotiated on the spot.

Contributor

Chris Doye has taught English in Europe, the Middle East, and the United States. She is now an associate professor in Japan.

What Do You Have?

Levels
Low intermediate +

Aims
Enrich and internalize
vocabulary through
communicative
cooperation
Discriminate between
verbs, adverbs,
adjectives, and nouns

Class Time
Variable

Preparation Time
35 minutes +

Resources
Pen and paper
Chalk and chalkboard or
pens and whiteboard
Work sheets with
columns for adjectives,
verbs, adverbs, and
nouns

Although this game is aimed at expanding students' ability to manipulate effectively adjectives, verbs, adverbs, and nouns, it also works as a beneficial tool for speaking in the target language. The teacher asks students to communicate in English while working on the production of words in small groups. This activity motivates students to enrich their vocabulary in a communicative way and engages them in a funny and competitive game.

Procedure

1. Write each letter in the English alphabet on a card and put them into a bag.
2. Create groups of three students.
3. Give each group a work sheet with assigned columns for adjectives, verbs, adverbs, and nouns.
4. Get one student from each group to draw 15 letters from the bag.
5. Ask students to form verbs, adjectives, adverbs, and nouns from their letters; they must write these words under the proper column of their work sheet. The more words they make, the more points they earn. They need to cooperate with their group members and communicate in English.
6. Set a time limit for the activity and write the finish time on the chalkboard or whiteboard.
7. Write each group's word lists under the group names on the chalkboard or whiteboard when time is up.

Caveats and Options

1. This game may be played as a follow-up activity after teaching nouns, adverbs, adverbs, and verbs, or you may focus on specific parts of speech.

2. When final lists of words are written on the chalkboard, students can exchange their words with classmates.
3. If the students' communicative ability is not sufficient to carry on the game in English, you may teach some words or structures that students might use in group work.
4. This activity may be used to teach words for situational language use. For instance, you may ask students to form adjectives, adverbs, and verbs related to an airport or library situation. When you have written the final lists on the chalkboard or whiteboard, ask the class for any additional associated words.

Contributor

Olga Tunaboylu Buyukyaruz is a doctoral student at the College of Education, Ohio State University, in the United States.

Give Me A Word That . . .

Levels
Intermediate

Aims
Enhance imagination
Activate passive
vocabulary

Class Time
30 minutes

Preparation Time
30 minutes

Resources
Index cards or slips of
paper

This activity involves students in a competition in which they use their repertoire of passive vocabulary.

Procedure

1. Prepare index cards (one for each student) with 15–20 vocabulary questions starting with the phrase "Give me a word that . . ." or "Give me a . . . word." For example:

Give me . . .	Give me a [...] word.
a word that dances.	[ballerina, Madonna]
a word that runs.	[runner, water, river]
a word that shines.	[sun, gold]
a word that bites.	[dog, cold]
a blue word.	[sky, sea]
a hot word.	[soup, sun, fire]
a wet word.	[water, juice, milk, rain]
a cold word.	[ice, winter, freezer]

2. Divide the class into groups of three.
3. Give each group a blank index card to keep score and three question cards (one for each student), and explain the activity:
    *   Student A in each group reads the questions on the index cards (e.g., *Give me a word that flies*).
    *   Students B and C compete to give a plausible answer in less than 30 seconds (e.g., B quickly says *plane*, and C follows with *bird*).
    *   Student A keeps score. The first correct answer gets 1 point. If the other student's answer is also correct, she gets half a point (e.g., 1 point for B in the example above and one half point for C).

● When A finishes the set of questions, students change roles until everyone has read the questions once.

4. Students begin playing the game. Have them play until someone reaches the championship.

Caveats and Options

1. Have students write their answers after saying them aloud, paying attention to spelling. If a word is misspelled, subtract half a point from the student's total score and give it to the student who corrects the spelling.

Contributor

Wisam Mansour is an assistant professor of English at the Applied Science University in Amman, Jordan.

A New Leaf

Levels
Intermediate +

Aims
Practice count/
noncount nouns and the
simple forms of verbs in
appropriate contexts

Class Time
30 minutes

Preparation Time
5 minutes

Resources
Chalkboard and chalk or
whiteboard and pens

Using correct noun and verb forms in a highly motivating communicative situation, students practice vocabulary to express their desires for self-improvement and to evaluate the self-improvement wishes of their classmates and teacher.

Procedure

1. Write on the chalkboard or whiteboard open-ended resolutions, such as the following:

   I am going to _____ every day.
   I am not going to _____ anymore.
   I am not going to spend so much money on _____.
   I am going to keep my _____ clean at all times.
   I am going to _____ more often.
   I am not going to _____ at home.
   I am going to give all my friends a _____.
   I am going to start looking for _____.

2. Tell students that they are going to turn over a new leaf—that is, make some changes in their lives that will make them better, happier people. Have them take out a sheet of paper and number it 1–8. After each number, they should write a word or expression that would fill in the blank in the resolution on the chalkboard or whiteboard corresponding to that number.

3. While the students are filling in the blanks, do the same on your own sheet of paper (not on the chalkboard or whiteboard).

4. When students have completed their lists of the eight fill-in-the-blanks, have them copy their answers—not the entire sentences—onto a separate piece of paper, but not in the original order. They

need to scramble the order of the answers. (You should put your answers in random order on the chalkboard or whiteboard while the students are doing this.)

5. Pair off students. Have partners exchange answer lists and, looking at their partner's list, try to guess which answer goes with which sentence by asking each other appropriate questions. For example:

Are you going to _____ every day?
Are you not going to _____ at home?

6. Students fill in the blank with their guess of the correct word or expression from the partner's list.

7. Tell students to write their partner's answers in order as they figure out each one. The first pair of students to come up with complete, correct lists for each other wins the first part of the game.

8. When all partners have completed this part of the game, the class will compete as partners to match your answers—written on the chalkboard or whiteboard—with the resolutions. Partners should take several minutes to agree on how they think you filled in the blanks and then write the answers in order.

9. Have one set of partners at a time read their guesses, and inform each pair of their success or failure after they finish reading the entire list. The first pair to match your list correctly to the blanks wins the game. Any other pairs that show they made the same choices may also win.

Caveats and Options

1. This game can be used around holiday time as a New Year's resolution game instead of just turning over a new leaf.

Contributor

Victoria Holder, an ESL instructor at San Francisco State University and San Francisco City College, in the United States, has recently published a teacher's resource book on practicing grammar without paper.

◆ Imparting and Seeking Factual Information
National Trivia

Levels
Any

Aims
Practice different
question forms

Class Time
20–30 minutes

Preparation Time
1 hour

Resources
Almanac
20–30 index cards
Four information sheets

Students swap trivia about countries in this small-group activity.

Procedure

1. Make four to six copies of almanac entries about four countries. Cut out the entries and mount them on index cards.
2. Develop an information sheet for each country (see Appendix). Select questions that ask for different kinds of information (e.g., numbers, names, cities, products, famous people).
3. Make enough packets for the entire class. Students in each small group will have a country card and an information sheet.
4. Put students into groups of four, with extra students dispersed throughout the groups, and give each student a country card and corresponding information sheet.
5. Instruct students to work in pairs to gather the information required and fill out the information sheet.
6. To complete the task, students talk to each of the other three students in the group and record the answers on the information sheet.

Caveats and Options

1. Choose countries of interest to the class. For example, in my Spanish classes, I have almanac entries about Argentina, Bolivia, Colombia, and Costa Rica.
2. For lower levels, provide students with complete questions. For more advanced classes, give students prompts that they use to develop their own questions.
3. As a follow-up, ask the class additional questions about the four countries or have students develop their own questions about the

other countries. (Be sure, however, that the questions can be answered with the almanac entries provided.)

4. For more advanced, motivated classes, assign a written summary or further research.

Appendix: Sample Information Sheets

This sample activity focused exclusively on numerical data. Only one question per country is given as an example.

Sheet 1

Your country: Argentina

Find out the information about these three countries:
Bolivia: What is the population?
Colombia: When did the Thousand-Day War begin?
Costa Rica: What is the average temperature in San José?

Sheet 2

Your country: Bolivia

Find out the information about these three countries:
Colombia: What is the area of the country?
Costa Rica: When did Oscar Arias win the Nobel Prize?
Argentina: When did Argentina declare its independence?

Sheet 3

Your country: Costa Rica

Find out the information about these three countries:
Argentina: What is the area of the country?
Colombia: What is the population of the largest city?
Bolivia: When was the author Prada Oropeza born?

Sheet 4

Your country: Colombia

Find out the information about these three countries:
Costa Rica: What is the population of the country?
Argentina: When did the Falkland Islands War take place?
Bolivia: What percent of the population is Quechua?

Contributor

Dennis Bricault is the director of ESL programs and an instructor in Spanish, at North Park College in Chicago, Illinois, in the United States. He has 17 years' teaching and administrative experience in Spain, Hungary, and the United States.

Memory Game

Levels
Any

Aims
Learn about classmates
in a communicative way

Class Time
30 minutes

Preparation Time
None

Resources
None

This challenging memory game offers students an opportunity to learn their classmates' names and other interesting information in a communicative situation. In addition, they practice speaking and listening skills and functions, such as asking for and giving information and clarification, and agreeing and disagreeing.

Procedure

1. Tell students that they will play a memory game and will have to listen carefully to their classmates.
2. Begin by modeling the information each student must supply (e.g., My name is Sally. I'm from the United States. I like Bruce Springsteen [or reading, dim sum, or baseball]).
3. Point to the first student in the first row, A, and ask A to give the same information about herself.
4. Point to the second student in the first row, B, and ask for the same information. Then ask B to recall the information about A. Other students can help, or B can ask questions if necessary.
5. Point to the third student, C, and ask C to talk about herself and then recall the information for both previous students. (In other words, it is a cumulative task.)
6. Continue through the end of the row, and then begin again with another row, so that no student will have to remember more than 8 or 10 names.
7. Encourage students to help each other so that the whole class is actively involved. As the game proceeds, begin to point randomly at any previous student or yourself to challenge the collective memory of the class.

8. When all the students have had a turn speaking, take the ultimate challenge. Can you remember all the students' names, homelands, and interests? Try—the students will help you.

Caveats and Options

1. Students at lower levels may need prompts written on the chalkboard or whiteboard.
2. The information students give can be varied to practice specific grammatical structures or vocabulary. For example, to practice past tense, students can tell what they did last weekend; to practice food items, they can name their favorite foods.

Contributor

Sally Winn teaches ESL at City College of San Francisco, in the United States.

Photographic Memory

Levels
Beginning +

Aims
Practice transnational
language skills in giving
information based on a
picture
Practice prepositions

Class Time
15 minutes

Preparation Time
Variable

Resources
Simply drawn pictures
of objects relevant to
students

This game incorporates elements of an information transfer activity and a memory test. It can also be used to practice supposition, confirmation, and clarification.

Procedure

1. Prepare a series of simple pictures relevant to your students.

2. Arrange students into groups of four or five.

3. Give a picture to one member of the group, Student A, and ask A to study it. It is very important that the other members of the group do not see the picture.

4. Collect the pictures. Then ask A to describe the picture to A's group members while each member tries to draw the picture from A's information. A must not tell the group the name of the object; A must only describe it. A then selects the best picture from A's group members and gives it to you.

5. Assign points to each group based on how closely the student's picture represents the actual picture. You can award the points or have the class vote. The procedure can then be repeated with different pictures.

Caveats and Options

1. With high-level students you may wish to use magazine pictures with more detail.

2. To involve students more in the game, ask them to draw the original pictures and then use them to play the game. For example, you could give the topic *furniture* and ask the class to draw an item of furniture.

Once this is done, the drawings are collected, and the groups are formed.

Contributor

Lindsay Miller is an assistant professor in the English Department at City University of Hong Kong.

What Does It Look Like?
How Does It Feel?

Levels
Beginning +

Aims
Use adjectives to
practice describing
things and people

Class Time
30 minutes

Preparation Time
1 hour

Resources
Picture and number
sheets

In this game, students expand their powers of description.

Procedure

1. Create two blank grids with the same number of cells. Draw pictures of things or people in each cell of one grid. Number each cell of the second grid. (You can control the level of difficulty with the pictures.)
2. Prepare a set of grids for each student. Cut out the pictures.
3. Pair off the students, giving each a set of pictures and a number sheet. Tell them it will be pair work and assign the roles of Student A and B, having pairs sit back-to-back so that they cannot see each other's desk.
4. Ask A in each pair to randomly place a picture on each cell of the number sheet.
5. Have A describe each picture using adjectives and without saying the name of the object (e.g., "Number 1. It is red and round."). B listens to the descriptions and places a picture matching A's description on the correct cell of the number sheet. Allow B to ask questions using different adjectives (e.g., "Is it delicious? Is it sweet?").
6. When A and B finish, tell them to check whether the order of the pictures is the same. Have A and B switch roles and repeat the procedure.

Appendix: Sample Grids

1	2	3
4	5	6
7	8	9
10	11	12

Contributor

Yasuko Takata is an instructor of Japanese in the Department of Linguistics at Ohio University, in the United States.

So Did I

Levels
Beginning +

Aims
Practice using the
simple past tense to
report things learners
have done recently

Class Time
10–15 minutes

Preparation Time
None

Resources
None

The object of the game is for students to discover something they did during a specified time period that no one else in the class did. It can be played using simple language structures and is a great warm-up activity for beginners who have basic vocabulary but may feel intimidated by an open-ended question such as, "Tell us what you did over the weekend."

Procedure

1. Have a learner report something she did during a specified time period, such as over the weekend (e.g., "I ate Italian food" or "I visited my grandmother").
2. Have each learner respond, in round robin fashion, with "I didn't" or "So did I." If anyone else says, "So did I," the learner must try again. The game continues until all learners have found something they did that was unique.

Caveats and Options

1. If the learners lack vocabulary or imagination, play a "three-strikes-and-you're-out" version: Each learner gets only three chances before moving on to the next player. This will avoid waiting on one person for too long.
2. For large groups, break the learners up into groups of four to six, tell them to play as many rounds as they can in a specified time, and then ask each group to report the most interesting thing done by one of their members.

Contributor

Jim Sick holds an MA in TESOL from Temple University Japan and currently teaches at Chuo University High School in Tokyo, Japan.

Ways of Seeing

Levels
Beginning +

Aims
Practice giving and
following instructions
Review geometrical
terms

Class Time
10-12 minutes

Preparation Time
None

Resources
Geometrical drawing

Caveats and Options

This is a classic information gap activity in which Student A has the information Student B wants. With the help of A's instructions, B draws four diagrams.

Procedure

1. Have students work in pairs. A has a copy of the geometrical drawing that is hidden from B. A gives B instructions for reproducing the diagrams in the boxes of the geometrical drawing (see the Appendix). B may ask for clarification.

2. Allow time for all students to complete their drawings. Students do not compare drawings until the task is over.

3. Explain that Picture 1 is how students see themselves; Picture 2 is how they see their home; Picture 3 is how they see their work or studies; Picture 4 is how they see their future.

1. Students can write a story, using the diagrams as prompts.

Acknowledgment

There are a number of variations of this psychology game. My colleague Mary Burns, at the International University of Japan summer school, showed me this version.

Appendix: Sample Geometrical Drawing

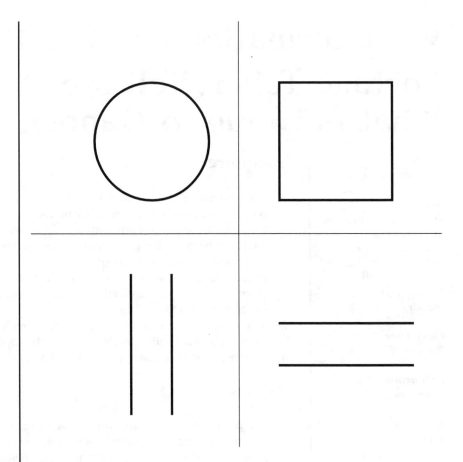

Contributor

Theresa Thiel is lecturer in the BEd TESL program in the Faculty of Education, University of Malaya, Kuala Lumpur, Malaysia.

◆ Confirmation and Clarification
Fortune Teller, Tell Me
What Is Going to Happen

Levels
Low intermediate +

Aims
Practice the future tense
in a communicative
situation
Make predictions and
ask for information
Practice reported
speech

Class Time
Variable

Preparation Time
5 minutes

Resources
Topic slips

Procedure

1. Put students in pairs and assign the role of fortune teller to one partner and customer to the other partner.
2. Give one topic slip to each customer and have the customer ask the fortune teller to make predictions about the topic. Have the fortune teller make as many predictions as possible about the customer's future regarding the topic (e.g., health, financial status). Allow the customer to ask for clarification and take brief notes while listening to the fortune teller.
3. At the end of the session, ask each customer to report to the class what the fortune teller predicted about the topic.
4. If there is still time, have the pairs exchange roles and topics.

Caveats and Options

1. The pairs can be given the same topic instead of different topics.
2. For students at a lower proficiency level, you can write the following prompts on the chalkboard or whiteboard before the game starts:

> Will I (be) . . . ?
>
> Am I going to (be) . . . ?
>
> You will (be) . . . .
>
> You are going to (be) . . . .
>
> The fortune teller said that I would (be) . . . .
>
> The fortune teller said that I was going to (be) . . . .

The fortune teller told me that I would (be) . . . .

The fortune teller told me that I was going to (be) . . . .

3. Skip the "reporting to the class" step (Step 3) if you only need to emphasize the future tense. If you need more of an emphasis on reported speech, the oral report can take the form of a written report based on the notes that the customer has taken.

Appendix: Sample Topic Slips

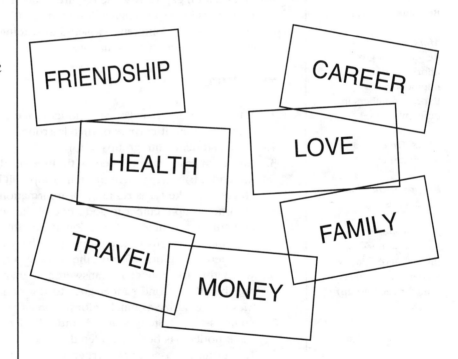

Contributor

Zubeyde Tezel is an EFL teacher and teacher trainer in Turkey. She is currently teaching at the American Language Institute, Indiana University of Pennsylvania, in the United States.

Just a Minute, I'll Check

Levels
Beginning–intermediate

Aims
Request and give
information using
numbers
Express numbers in
different ways

Class Time
45–60 minutes

Preparation Time
45 minutes

Resources
For Sale notices for
three different items
Student work sheets
(one for each group)

This information gap relay game requires students to read For Sale signs and ask questions to exchange information. It gives students practice expressing numbers in different ways and in reading, giving, and listening for numbers used in everyday situations.

Procedure

1. Make three different For Sale notices (see Appendix A) and tape them in different corners of the classroom.
2. Divide students into groups of three.
3. Give each group a work sheet with three blank For Sale notices (see Appendix B). One student in each group will be the writer, and the others will take turns running for information.
4. Ask one group member to go to one of the For Sale notices and try to memorize as much information as possible.
5. The runner returns to the group, and the writer asks questions to complete the information on the work sheet.
6. When the first runner has answered as many of the questions as possible, the second runner goes to the same For Sale notice and tries to memorize as much information as possible.
7. Runners repeat Steps 4 and 5 until all of the information on the blank notice has been completed.
8. The group chooses a new writer and repeats Steps 4 and 5 for the second sale item. When they have completed the second blank notice, they repeat the procedure for the third item.
9. When students have completed the three For Sale notices and are sure their numbers are correct, they should shout, *Finished*. You can then stop the game or let other groups continue until everyone is finished, noting the order in which groups finish.

10. To find out the winner, ask the team that finished first the questions and have them give their answers. If any answers are incorrect, move on to the team that finished next. The first team with all the correct answers is the winner.

Caveats and Options

1. To complete this activity, students must be familiar with different ways of expressing numbers and have been previously taught the questions for eliciting information from their teammates.
2. Students may need to be reminded to ask for clarification and confirmation. Some useful prompts include repeating what the speaker just said (e.g., "Sorry, could you repeat that? Did you say _____?") or, if students can't remember the information, saying, "Sorry, I don't know" or "Just a minute, I'll check."

Appendix A: Sample For Sale Notice

FOR SALE	
ITEM:	Mercedes Benz
YEAR:	1982
YEARS OLD:	14 years
PRICE:	$45,000
ADDRESS:	313 W. 30th Ave.
APARTMENT:	1330
PHONE:	365-7982

Appendix B: Sample Blank Work Sheet

STUDENT WORKSHEET

ITEM:

YEAR:

YEARS OLD:

PRICE:

ADDRESS:

APARTMENT:

PHONE:

Acknowledgment

A special thanks to Eric Bray and Chris Ford for their helpful comments.

Contributor

Robin Russ has taught in Australia and Spain and currently teaches at Kansai University in Osaka, Japan.

◆ Expressing Emotional Attitudes

What Will You Do With This?

Levels
High beginning-
intermediate

Aims
Practice and reinforce
the use of the auxilliary
will

Class Time
10–15 minutes

Preparation Time
1 hour +

Resources
Pictures prepared in
advance on overhead
transparencies (OHTs)
or posters
Word cards
Instructions

Procedure

1. Put students into groups and warm them up with a quick activity involving the future tense. For example, you could say, "When I'm old I'll be . . . ," and ask students to continue (e.g., "When I'm old I'll be bad-tempered; when I'm bad-tempered I'll get cross with people; when I get cross I'll . . . ").
2. Give instructions for the game (see Appendix A).
3. Show a picture (Appendix B) and a chosen word card (see Appendix C). Give students a few moments to think and discuss the question, then ask two groups for contributions. The remaining group(s) act as judges of group responses. Keep the game moving at a brisk pace.
4. Keep score, or get one of the students to do so, or find some other way of inducing a lively, competitive yet playful spirit.

Caveats and Options

1. You can introduce other factors such as degrees of formality (e.g., *I will, I shall, I'll*). Vary the responses by having students use the second or third person or plurals (e.g., introduce another picture with a person or people on it or point to a person or group in the classroom).
2. Impose restrictions on the type of answer required (e.g., the shortest, the longest, the funniest, the most unusual).
3. Extend this to other tenses, such as the future progressive, *I'm going to . . . .*

References and Further Reading

Byrne, D. (1986). *Teaching oral English*. Harlow, England: Longman.

Jones, L. (1992). *Communicative grammar practice*. Cambridge: Cambridge University Press.

Wright, A. (1984). *One thousand pictures for teachers to copy*. London: Collins.

Appendix A: Sample Rules

1. Tell students that they will see a picture and a word. The object in the picture is a present to them, and the word describes how they feel when they receive it.
2. Ask students to tell the class what they will do with the object because of the way they feel about it (e.g., "I will ride it to town," "I will put it in a cupboard"). Their response will be judged by the other groups according to
   - how easy it is to understand
   - correct use of the future tense
   - how original or funny or interesting it is

Appendix B: Sample Pictures

Appendix C: Sample Word Cards

Contributors

Rex Berridge, teacher educator, is at the English Language Unit, University of Wales, in the United Kingdom. Jenny Muzambindo, teacher educator and specialist in English teaching and the methodology of teaching across the curriculum, is head of Communication Skills, at Gweru Teachers' College, in Zimbabwe.

The Situation Game

Levels
Intermediate +

Aims
Become aware of levels
of politeness required in
different conversational
situations
Practice language skills
associated with a range
of language functions

Class Time
2–3 hours over several
sessions

Preparation Time
1 hour

Resources
Pictures depicting
people conversing in
varied settings and with
varied levels of formality
Index cards
Situation titles in a cup
Vocabulary sheet with
useful expressions

This situation game provides meaningful, context-oriented speaking practice that reflects communicative situations students will encounter as they try out their language skills in the community. This activity often stimulates vocabulary development and discussion as well as a sharing of problem situations among class members.

Procedure

1. Examine pictures and brainstorm to elicit who the people in the pictures are, what the problem is they are discussing, and what level of politeness (high, medium, low) is probably being used.
2. Put students into pairs and ask them to describe a recent situation in which they had to resolve a problem. After verbally describing the situation to their partner, ask that each write on an index card the number of people involved, a description of the speakers and situation, and the level of politeness required (see the Appendix).
3. Edit and clarify student-generated situation cards in preparation.
4. While students are working in pairs, work with another teacher or one of the more proficient students and prepare to role-play a situation. Ask students to note the problem and communication used to express the level of politeness. Note that politeness can be communicated both verbally and nonverbally.
5. Role-play a situation. Debrief, listing politeness techniques on the board and eliciting, "How did you feel when I . . ." from the other speaker, sharing how the conversation felt from the speakers' point of view. If there is enough time, role-play again, using a different level of politeness. Debrief, eliciting things to consider when deciding appropriate politeness (formality of situation, status, age, culture, and cost of solution).

6. Ask that each student draw the title of a situation to role-play. With their partner, students must decide on the level of politeness and practice role-playing the situation so that they can present it to the class the next day.

Caveats and Options

1. It is important to keep the activity lighthearted and stress-free and to discourage memorized or script-driven role plays. Avoid giving help to the actors as the situation is being played; one important part of being able to converse in a second language is being able to circumlocute when you cannot find a word or expression.
2. Video clips could be used more effectively than pictures in Step 1. As an additional component of Step 3, you may ask students to edit the cards before editing them yourself.
3. Consider videotaping the rehearsed role plays so that students can scritique themselves and so that you can use the videotapes as examples for future classes. You could take an additional class day to review the videotape and to work with the class on language improvement. Alternatively, meet with each role play group separately to review the tape and discuss language needs.

Appendix: Sample Situation Cards

Card 1: Bicycle Rental (three persons)

Speakers: Two bicycle riders, one bicycle renter

Situation: You rent two bicycles for 4 hours, planning to have a picnic and ride bicycles all afternoon on Sunday. You ride for 1 hour and your bicycles break down. You return (on foot) to the rental location, angry, hot, and tired. You insist that the renter give you your money back. The renter insists on keeping the money you paid for 4 hours of riding time.

Politeness: Low

Card 2: The Movie (two-three persons)

Speakers: Salesperson at the ticket counter, moviegoer(s)

Situation: You make a special trip to the movie theater in the early afternoon to buy tickets for the 8 p.m. show. When you arrive at 7:45 p.m. to attend the show, the salesperson tells you the sign was wrong. The show really started at 7:30 p.m. With your companion, decide what to do and get the salesperson to agree.

Politeness: Medium

Card 3: The Ferry (three-five persons)

Speakers: A noisy group, playing a radio loudly as they play a card game together, and a tired, quiet group

Situation: Ask the noisy group to turn down their music. Explain that they are too loud. They are bothering everybody on the ferry. As you talk with them, you learn also that they are from your university (or school or neighborhood). Decide whether to make friends and join groups.

Politeness: Medium

Card 4: The Telephone Call (two persons)

Speakers: Two roommates

Situation: You have been expecting a very important telephone call. When it finally comes, you are not at home. Your roommate answered the telephone, but does not tell you about the call until now. Express your frustration and, with your roommate, decide what to do about this problem.

Politeness: Medium

Card 5: Parents' Day (four persons)

Speakers: Student, parents, and Professor Smith, from your major subject area, with whom you have had two classes

Situation: You and your parents are touring campus on Parents' Day when you run into Professor Smith, who is somewhat long-winded. Professor Smith is interested in meeting with and talking to your parents. Your parents are concerned about catching their train on time. They must return home to take care of your young niece after school.

Politeness: High

Card 6: The Computer Conference (three persons)

Speakers: Mr. Lawrence, specialist for a computer firm who just gave a presentation; Mr. Reed, assistant to Mr. Lawrence; Mr. Stephens, friend of Mr. Reed

Situation: Between presentations, tea is served. Mr. Reed and Mr. Stephens are chatting near the tea table and trying to quickly decide dinner plans when Mr. Lawrence approaches and interrupts before plans can be finalized.

Politeness: High

Card 7: Bad Shoes (two persons)

Speakers: Shopkeeper and customer

Situation: You bought a pair of very expensive shoes last week. You had saved for 3 months to buy these shoes. After wearing them for only a week, they fall apart. Take them back to the shopkeeper. Demand a new pair and a guarantee that the new pair will not fall apart.

Politeness: Medium

Card 8: The Scholarship (three persons)

Speakers: Jim Brown, student applying for a master's degree in business administration and hoping for a 2-year scholarship; Dr. Andrews, chairperson of the scholarship committee; Dr. Andrews' secretary.

Situation: You arrive for your interview with the scholarship committee, which consists of Dr. Andrews and Dr. Adams. Approach the secretary, introduce yourself, and explain why you are there. The secretary asks you to take a seat, calls Dr. Andrews on the telephone, and he appears and greets you. You chat with him and the secretary while waiting for another professor, Dr. Adams, to arrive. Dr. Adams never appears, however.

Politeness: High

Contributor

Kim Hughes Wilhelm taught ESL in Hong Kong and Malaysia and is currently Intensive English Program curriculum coordinator and assistant professor of linguistics at Southern Illinois University, in the United States.

Part IV: Developing
Skills in Discourse

Editors' Note

The activities in this section develop discourse competence. Students must combine their knowledge of grammatical forms with meanings to achieve a coherent spoken or written text within a particular genre. The activities incorporate many of the skills practiced in the earlier part of this book and move students toward the effective, meaningful, and appropriate use of language to facilitate communication. They emphasize cohesion and coherence skills in speech and in writing, including the use of appropriate grammatical features such as pronouns and conjunctions, and text organization skills, such as constructing a clear sequence of events or facilitating the smooth transition of ideas between sentences and paragraphs.

Most of the activities require collaboration, enabling learners to pool their linguistic and content knowledge to make a complete text. They also involve discourse in everyday communicative situations that demand extended knowledge of interviewing and conversational skills, as well as the oral construction of collaborative stories. Collaborative stories with a writing outcome are also featured in this section, as are five activities allowing students to practice specific grammatical skills that are useful in discourse.

◆ Conducting Interviews and Conversations

Got It in One

Levels
Beginning

Aims
Review conversation
openers and their
appropriate responses

Class Time
10–15 minutes

Preparation Time
30 minutes

Resources
Openers and responses
written on separate
strips

Working against the clock, students try to match as many openers as
they can with an appropriate response.

Procedure

1. Have all students except one sit in a circle. Give the seated students a
   strip with a response (see the Appendix) and have them read and
   memorize it. You may wish to allow them to refer to the strip during
   the game, depending on confidence and ability levels.
2. Have one student stand in the center of the circle and call out an
   opener (again, see the Appendix). The seated student who thinks she
   has the appropriate response calls it out and hands her strip to the
   center student.
3. The center student sees how many strips he can collect in 2 minutes
   or the amount of time it takes to match all openers and responses.

Caveats and Options

1. This activity also works well with pairs. Student A is given the openers
   and Student B has the responses. See how many they can match
   within the allotted time or how long it takes to match them all.
2. A more demanding variation is to place two students in the center.
   The seated students call out their responses and the center students
   try to memorize who said what. Students then take turns calling out
   an opener and trying to match it with a response, while also
   identifying the speaker. The seated student only speaks if the center
   student is correct. Points are scored for each correct identification.

Appendix: Sample Opener and Response Strips

Opener: You're a lucky man!	Response: Don't I know it.
Opener: This cake is delicious.	Response: Thanks, I'm glad you like it.
Opener: Well done. I heard you got your license.	Response: Thanks, I never thought I'd make it.
Opener: Congratulations on the new arrival.	Response: Thanks. Isn't she adorable?

Contributor

Geraldine Hetherton is an EFL lecturer at Fukui Prefectural University, in Japan, and has also taught in Europe, Africa, and the Middle East.

Scavenge for Answers

Levels
Intermediate +

Aims
Practice communicative
skills in an authentic
situation
Learn new vocabulary

Class Time
Variable

Preparation Time
15-30 minutes

Resources
One or more questions
concerning the English
language

By seeking information from speakers of English outside the classroom, students broaden their communicative experience. Their need to initiate a conversation and to understand the information they receive makes this a high-stakes activity that heightens their motivation.

Procedure

1. Prepare a list of idioms or slang, loan words, homonyms, or even gestures. Ask students to interview speakers of English to find out the meanings of the items on their list.
2. Have students present their results to their classmates.

Caveats and Options

1. Depending on their level and the time available, students may be given one or several questions. The question or questions may be the same for all students or different.
2. If the class meets in a primarily English-speaking environment—as opposed to an EFL environment—a general topic (e.g., idioms) may be assigned rather than a list of specific examples of that topic. Students then collect from their respondents examples and their meanings.
3. The game is even more challenging if themes are used. For example, with an idioms theme, you could stipulate that all examples contain parts of the body or colors.
4. Students may need to practice their interviewing skills with each other before seeking out other speakers of English.
5. Partners or small groups may compare results, or individuals may present their results to the class.

6. Students may gather information as class work or homework, and you may need to set a time limit.

Contributor

Jeannine Dobbs has taught ESL at Harvard University, Northern Essex Community College, New Hampshire College, and Bradford College, in the United States.

Give Us a Clue

Levels
Intermediate

Aims
Review socially
appropriate responses

Class Time
20-30 minutes

Preparation Time
30-50 minutes

Resources
Crossword puzzle
12 question cards
Dice

In this activity students work in pairs or in groups of up to six people. The throw of the dice determines the crossword puzzle clue the student will choose to answer. The object of the game is to complete all 12 clues on the crossword. Because students hear each other's responses, the content area is reinforced.

Procedure

1. Divide the class into pairs or groups and distribute a crossword puzzle to each student.
2. Give each pair or group a pair of dice and a set of 12 question cards (see Appendix A) divided into horizontal and vertical clues.
3. The members of each group throw the dice to decide the order of play (e.g., the person who throws the highest score goes first). The first player, A, throws the dice and chooses a horizontal or vertical card. If A answers the question correctly, A writes that answer on the crossword puzzle (see Appendix B). If A cannot answer, play moves to the second player. In this way students take turns throwing the dice, choosing and answering questions, and filling in their crossword. If a player throws a 4 and has previously completed 4 horizontal and 4 vertical, that player must skip that turn and pass play to the next player.
4. The first student to complete all 12 clues is the winner.

Caveats and Options

1. This game can also be played with an individual: The teacher calls out the appropriate question and the student tries to answer. In this case there is no need for question cards. Because there is no competitor, the student could play against the clock, seeing how long it takes to complete the crossword.

2. As an alternative to the question cards you can appoint a question master to each group and provide this person with a question and answer sheet. The question master calls out the relevant question when the players throw the dice.

3. A crossword can be devised to cover any topic appropriate to your students. The level of difficulty can be increased or decreased by adapting the clues.

Appendix A: Sample Question Card

3. Down
   What do Americans say at Halloween?

Appendix B: Sample Crossword Puzzle

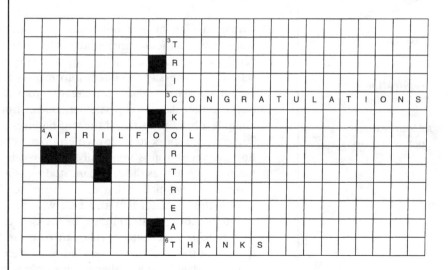

Contributor

Geraldine Hetherton is an EFL lecturer at Fukui Prefectural University, in Japan, and has also taught in Europe, Africa, and the Middle East.

Coherence and Clarity

Levels
Low intermediate +

Aims
Develop group
communication skills
Collect and organize
data
Develop brevity and
clarity in report and
essay writing

Class Time
1 hour

Preparation Time
20-30 minutes

Resources
Copy of the task

This activity is a good icebreaker with new classes. It can be used to practice oral and written communication skills and as preparation for questionnaire design or report or essay writing. The task only works if messages are conveyed between groups in clear, succinct, and accurate prose. It is also a useful activity for introducing students to group work and raising their awareness of effective group organization and problem solving. The time factor adds urgency and excitement.

Procedure

1. Divide class into at least four groups (e.g., A, B, C, D or red, green, blue, yellow), with at least three students in each.
2. Set the scene: Each group is a team of consultants employed by the school or university to collect information about students' habits as part of a plan to build a new recreation room for students. Each group has to gather data on a particular subject from all the other groups, compile a brief report, and present findings to the class.
3. Students can speak to their own group members, but all communication between groups must only be in writing and delivered by the teacher, who acts as the mailman. Students should raise their hands to show they have mail to deliver and must clearly address all messages.
4. Inform the students that the task will be run on strict time constraints—about 30-40 minutes for the data collection and writing.
5. Distribute the task sheet. This can take the form of a brief memo specifying the information needed. Each sheet should ask the group to collect data from all other groups on a particular topic, such as:
   ● favorite TV programs
   ● daily drinks and beverages
   ● magazines and newspapers typically read

- typical evening entertainment
- snacks and sweets normally consumed
- type of music habitually enjoyed
- the last six movies seen

6. Leave the activity in the students' hands as they design brief questionnaires, respond to the questions of other groups, clarify ambiguities, and write a brief essay or presentation. The teacher's role is to deliver mail and constantly remind students of the time remaining.
7. Groups can then present their findings either orally or in a brief essay.

Caveats and Options

1. Although the activity works best if timing is strictly controlled, removing this constraint allows students to produce more accurate work and a better final product.
2. Oral presentations should allow students to present their findings on an overhead transparency. Teachers may like to debrief students by focusing on the task itself, asking students to explain their difficulties and approaches to the activity. This should emphasize the importance of brevity, clarity, and directness in the communications.
3. In more advanced classes, teachers can discuss some of the problems and advantages of working in groups (e.g., how students arrived at decisions, resolved conflicts, or prevented one member from dominating the group) and how strategies might be improved (e.g., ideal group size; specialized roles, such as chair and secretary; seating arrangements; or diplomatic language).

Contributor

Ken Hyland is associate professor at City University of Hong Kong.

◆ Collaborative Storytelling: Speaking

Spontaneous Oral Development of Group Stories

Levels
Any

Aims
Use competition as a stimulus in composing an oral story

Class Time
20-30 minutes

Preparation Time
None

Resources
Writing paper and pencils

The competitive atmosphere of this activity is exciting for children and allows them to speak in the L2 without fear of making mistakes. The context of the small group is nonthreatening, and children know they have the support of others in the group. Because the children are learning to evaluate the stories of the other groups, they in turn learn to be more discerning in the development of their own stories. The winning stories, when prepared in small book format, make excellent reading material for the classroom and are eagerly read during free reading periods.

Procedure

1. Seat children in groups and give them a number corresponding with the order of their sentence in the story and the topic for their group story. The number of the children in the group will vary with their level. With younger children, you could have three students in each group; with older students, six to eight children.
2. The first child gives the opening sentence of the story as quickly as possible. Other children in the group may help the child with the sentence or make suggestions to improve the sentence. The second child suggests the second sentence; others in the group can help the child.
3. Before the third child starts the third sentence, the first two children repeat their sentences in order so that the sequence in the development of the story is clear to the third child. The third sentence is then given with the help of other group members if necessary.

4. Repeat this pattern until all group members have contributed their sentences.

5. When the story is complete, the group calls, "Ready." A scribe on behalf of the group starts copying the story while students wait for other groups to complete their stories. When all groups are ready, they tell their stories to the rest of the class, with each child in the group repeating his sentence.

6. Award points on the following basis: If there have been five groups competing, the first group finished scores 5 points, and the last group finished scores 1 point.

7. Groups vote on the quality of the stories. Each group awards the other groups 1–5 points for each of the following criteria: how interesting the story was; how effective the sequence, development, and conclusion were; how well vocabulary and expression were used.

8. Give the winning group a small reward. If the activity is repeated the following week, use a different grouping system to avoid having the same group of children always winning.

9. Copy stories on sheets of paper, illustrated, and displayed in the classroom. The teacher usually types the winning story, making any necessary corrections and adjustments, has it illustrated, and presents it to the class in small book format.

Contributor

Lewis Larking teaches at Central Queensland University, in Australia.

Amazing Answers

Levels
Low intermediate +

Aims
Develop creativity in
language thought and
use

Class Time
Variable

Preparation Time
10 minutes +

Resources
Question and answer
strips

This is a problem-solving game that puts learners in a position to focus on the immense variety of possibilities in language (e.g., use of clauses and creative vocabulary) in a relaxed and enjoyable setting. If students play individually, internal thought processes figure heavily; if they play in pairs or teams, more overt communicative processes are also addressed.

Procedure

1. Ask the students to sit around a large table or cluster of tables. Place the question strips (see Appendix A) face down and spread out on one area of the table, and the answer strips (see Appendix B) likewise in another area of the table.
2. Have one student select a question strip, turn it over, and read it aloud (e.g., "What is your favorite sport?"). Have another student select an answer strip and turn it over. Ask the student to read the answer word aloud and make a sentence that plausibly answers the question (e.g., "hamburger . . . What I like best is playing tennis while eating a hamburger.").
3. Continue until all the strips have been used or every student has had a chance to participate.

Caveats and Options

1. Teachers or students can prepare additional strips that could focus, for example, on the relevant language or discussion themes addressed in their classrooms.
2. Teams could be formed, with points awarded for effort, creativity, speed, or correct grammar.
3. The best answers could be used to launch other spoken or written activities.

Appendix A: Sample Question Strips

1. What did you do last night?

2. What is in your bedroom?

3. Who is your favorite singer?

4. What are you going to do next weekend?

5. Where did you go on your last vacation?

6. What does your father do?

7. How do you play tennis?

8. Where do you live?

9. What kind of food do you like?

10. What's your best friend like?

11. What kind of job would you like to have?

12. What is your mother's name?

13. What would you do if you had a lot of money?

14. What are you studying now?

15. What's your favorite sport?

16. What did you eat for breakfast?

17. Where did you go last night?

18. What is your father's first name?

19. How would you describe your personality?

20. What does your best friend look like?

21. What will you drink later?

22. Why are you studying English?

23. Who did you meet yesterday?

24. What do you have in your bag?

25. What is the most important thing in your life?

Appendix B: Sample Answer Strips

Tom Cruise	hamburgers	Australia	Madonna
snakes	terrible	London	t-shirt
volleyball	shy	restaurant	pencils
rabbit	businessman	beautiful	money
potato	exciting	Bryan Adams	English
Mary	smell	lemonade	crazy
slow			

Contributor

Richard Humphries is an ESL lecturer at Kansai Gaidai College, in Japan.

Unmix and Match

Levels
Intermediate

Aims
Identify the logical
sequence of a story

Class Time
20 minutes

Preparation Time
30 minutes

Resources
Comic strip story

Many people enjoy comic strip stories. This activity draws on that enjoyment and exploits the fun of comics to give students practice in matching dialogue and image and in ordering the resultant pairs to form a logically sequenced story line.

Procedure

1. Cut a comic strip story into individual pictures. Remove the dialogue.
2. Divide the class into two groups, A and B. Give each student in Group A a picture from the story and distribute the dialogue among the members of Group B.
3. The students mingle and try to match the pictures and the dialogue. When the students are satisfied with their matches, members of A sit with their dialogue partners from B.
4. The pair who think they have the first picture in the story sequence display it and read the dialogue, or you can indicate who holds the first picture.
5. Those who think they have the second picture then display it, read the second dialogue, and sit beside the first pair.
6. Pairs continue to reconstruct the story in this manner until the complete story has been reassembled.

Caveats and Options

1. With larger classes or more able students, you could distribute three or more comic strip stories randomly. The first group to assemble their story correctly is the winner.

Contributor

Geraldine Hetherton is an EFL lecturer at Fukui Prefectural University, in Japan, and has taught in Europe, Africa, and the Middle East.

Picture That!

Levels
Low intermediate +

Aims
Describe pictures
accurately
Listen to details in
descriptions
Ask questions to elicit
further information

Class Time
30–40 minutes

Preparation Time
30 minutes

Resources
Sets of four or five
pictures showing a
development of events
Chalkboard or
whiteboard and chalk or
pens

Students arrange a set of jumbled pictures so that they form a coherent story. Students have to do this without showing their pictures to the other people in the group. They also have to compose a story orally in groups.

Procedure

1. Prepare the sets of pictures:
   - Select suitable pictures such as cartoon strips or those used in picture compositions.
   - Write a letter on each frame to indicate its place in the sequence.
   - Make enough sets of these pictures for the number of groups you have.
   - Cut out each frame and mount it on a small piece of card (this is optional, but you can then recycle your pictures with other classes).
2. In class, divide students into groups of four or five, according to the number of pictures you have in a set.
3. Instruct students to assign a letter to each member in the group. Distribute one picture to each student in a group according to their letters (i.e., Student A receives Picture A and Student B receives Picture B).
4. Instruct students not to show their pictures to other people in the group. Once students have each received a picture, tell them to decide on a logical arrangement of these pictures to create a coherent story. Tell them that they are not allowed to see one another's pictures and that everything should be done orally. You can leave them to decide how to approach the task. Alternatively, you could advise them to begin by taking turns describing the picture they each have.

5. Give students 20 minutes for this task, advising them that they must then tell their story to the class. Each student will have to tell the part of the story depicted by the picture the student has.
6. Once time is up, get each group to take turns telling their stories. The student with the picture that begins the story starts, followed by the others in the group. Once they have finished, write on the chalkboard or whiteboard the sequence decided by that particular group (e.g., B, C, A, D). After this, repeat the process with another group until they all have had a chance to tell their stories.
7. Tell students to lay their pictures on the table according to their agreed sequence. You may want to give them a few minutes to discuss what they see.
8. Announce the sequence in the original set of pictures and compare this with those decided by the different groups.
9. The group whose sequence matches or is closest to the original is the winner. Alternatively, you may want to get the class to vote for the most interesting and convincing story.

Caveats and Options

1. If using cartoon strips, choose only those that show a clear development of events (some cartoon strips rely on words and show very few differences in each frame).
2. As an additional task, you can ask each group to give a title to their story.

Contributors

Christine C. M. Goh and Cheah Yin Mee are lecturers in the School of Arts, National Institute of Education, Nanyang Technological University, in Singapore. Goh is interested in the teaching of oral communication skills for general and academic purposes. Cheah's interests are in language and literacy education at the primary level.

Add a Word

This activity is simple and moves quickly. It develops the ability of students to comprehend which part of speech is needed at a particular point in a sentence and helps them concentrate on building larger and more complex sentences.

Procedure

1. Ask all the students to stand up. Explain that you will begin a sentence with a single word. One by one, each standing student is to add another word to the sentence to make it longer.
2. Each student should be given roughly 10 seconds to respond or sit.
3. Follow the action by writing the sentence as it develops on the chalkboard or whiteboard. Ask the class whether an answer is acceptable, mediating when necessary.
4. If the student adds a word that is possible, the student may remain standing. If the word added by a student is wrong, the student is out and sits down.
5. If the sentence is at an obvious end, a new sentence may begin. To make this new sentence as challenging as the first, make the topic relate to the first sentence.
6. The last remaining student who correctly adds a word and remains standing is the winner. If the final two students standing both answer incorrectly, then the game may be called a tie.

Caveats and Options

1. This activity works best with a small class (15 or fewer). It may be done with larger classes, allotting additional time for the activity.
2. A point in a sentence that requires a difficult part of speech (e.g., verb phrase, particular tense) can quickly eliminate students.

3. An additional option is to have each student read the sentence aloud before adding a word. This gives the student additional time to decide what possible word to add.

Contributor

Shawn M. Clankie has taught in the United States and Japan, and is currently in the graduate program in linguistics at the University of Cambridge, in the United Kingdom.

◆ Collaborative Storytelling: Writing Tapeworm Story

Levels
High beginning +

Aims
Overcome the fear of writing in the L2
Focus on content rather than on form when writing the first draft of a text
Develop a more positive attitude toward the writing process in general

Class Time
Usually 15–30 minutes for a two-page story

Preparation Time
5 minutes

Resources
Chalkboard, whiteboard, or overhead projector (OHP) and chalk or pens
Several sheets of oversized blank paper

This is an associative activity, in which students work together to create a text.

Procedure

1. Have the class brainstorm character outlines, locations, and other features of the tapeworm story: One student goes to the chalkboard, whiteboard, or OHP and writes down a name or location; other students follow, expanding on each other's ideas, words, and phrases until a rough web of ideas for a potential story is created.
2. Ask all students to look briefly at the whole-class associative activity again.
3. Split the class into groups of five maximum. Distribute the paper to the groups and give each group one pen.
4. Explain the rules of the game. Tell the groups that they have 30 minutes to create a story as a group, using ideas, thoughts, and concepts from the whole-class activity
   - the first student, A, must give the pen to the second student, B, after A thinks she has created a meaningful unit, such as a phrase, sentence, two sentences, or a short paragraph
   - A should spend no more than 5 minutes creating the first unit
   - B should scan A's text and continue the story by adding meaningful information anywhere in it
   - B should then pass the text to the third student, C, who scans the newly created text and continues the story in the same way

5. Have students play the game until all of the members in each group have had a chance to contribute to the piece and feel that a story has been created.
6. Have each group exchange texts with another group, scan them, and discuss questions with members of the other group. Groups can make suggestions to improve the flow of the story.
7. Ask students to share stories as a whole-class activity, mentioning at least five details from each story.

Caveats and Options

1. Ask students to bring to class pictures, photos, or cartoons from magazines or newspapers and use the situations in them to generate ideas for the tapeworm stories.
2. Give students index cards and have different students write names and descriptions of characters, locations, or a time periods. Then have student groups randomly pick several characters, two or three locations, and one or two time periods to incorporate into their story before groups start their activity.
3. Have students, especially in more advanced classes, compose their tapeworm stories in pairs.
4. Start a student magazine to publish the edited versions of the tapeworm stories. This gives a wider audience access to them and lets students feel that they have accomplished something.

References and Further Reading

Becker, C. A. (1991). *Quantity and quality of writing in early acquisition: A case for "associative activities" in foreign language classes*. Los Angeles: University of Southern California.

Rico, G. L. (1983). *Writing the natural way: Using right-brain techniques to release your expressive powers*. Los Angeles: Tarcher.

Contributor

Claudia Becker teaches intermediate and advanced academic writing classes for international students as well as tests and places students in the English as a Second and International Language Program at Loyola University Chicago. Her research areas include free writing in the initial stages of foreign language acquisition, sociolinguistic aspects of German in the work place, and spoken versus written language proficiency.

Narrow It Down

Levels
Low intermediate +

Aims
Write narrow topic
sentences and thesis
statements
Think quickly in English
Work cooperatively

Class Time
Variable

Preparation Time
5–10 minutes

Resources
Lined index cards
Fastener (e.g., tape,
glue)

This game focuses on the task of narrowing topics and theses, but does so in an environment where discussion with peers and brainstorming are vital. It involves reading, writing, listening, and speaking skills as well as grammar, and is a lively way to assist students in accomplishing a task that is often tedious, time-consuming, and frustrating for them.

Procedure

1. Review reasons for and techniques of narrowing topic sentences or thesis statements.
2. Create a topic card for each team. You can use student journals and writing samples to help determine topics that interest learners. Each card should have a single broad topic written at the top. Number the cards.
3. Tape the topic cards to walls in the classroom, leaving enough room between them that the writing cannot be seen from the next card or from seats in the room.
4. Divide the learners into pairs or teams.
5. Assign each team to start with a different topic card. One learner from each team, A, must read the assigned card and return to the team to report on its topic. The team will narrow the topic and A will write it in grammatically correct form on the topic card. Each team who writes a grammatically correct narrowed topic sentence within the allotted time earns 1 point for that round.
6. Assign each team to another topic card that will have the original topic and a narrower topic sentence developed by another team, and repeat the process. After several rounds, the card may have several topic sentences on it (see the Appendix).

7. Finish with a discussion of the process, relating it to other writing assignments in class.

Caveats and Options

1. The teacher, class, or judges can evaluate the narrowed topic sentences after each round. If the sentence is incorrect in some way, it can be corrected or removed.
2. Having the topic card taped to the wall provides an opportunity for different learners to report to the team and write the finished product on the index card. An alternative is to have the topics on pieces of paper that would be passed from team to team at the end of each round.
3. After the original topics have been narrowed, put the learners into large groups and give each group three of the original topic cards. Each group must develop a thesis statement from the narrowed topic sentences on their three cards, as if they were to write one essay containing paragraphs for which these were the topic sentences. After the allotted time, pass the cards to a different group, until all of the large groups have developed thesis statements for each set of cards. Award points, if desired, for the best thesis statements for each set of cards.

References and Further Reading

Frydenberg, G., & Boardman, C. (1990). *You're in charge: Writing to communicate.* New York: Addison-Wesley.

Oshima, A., & Hogue, A. (1991). *Writing academic English.* New York: Addison-Wesley.

Smalley, R., & Ruetten, M. (1995). *Refining composition skills: Rhetoric and grammar.* Boston: Heinle & Heinle.

Appendix: Sample Topic Card

Drugs
Alcohol is a drug.
Alcohol is a dangerous drug.
The effects of alcohol are dangerous.
The effects of alcohol on driving ability make it a dangerous drug.

Contributor

Joy Egbert teaches at Indiana University in Bloomington, Indiana, in the United States.

Chinese Whispers in Writing

Levels
Intermediate

Aims
Develop discourse skills
in writing
Use oral language to
negotiate and contribute
in a group writing
activity

Class Time
30 minutes +

Preparation Time
None

Resources
One piece of paper for
each group of four or
five students

Contributor

This communicative game allows students to practice writing single sentences and use their knowledge of cohesive devices to put together an integrated and creative piece of work.

Procedure

1. Place students in groups of four or five. Give each group a blank piece of paper. Have one member of the group, A, write a sentence, fold the paper over the top of the sentence so the next person cannot read it, and pass the paper to the left.
2. The next group member, B, writes a sentence, folds the paper over it, and passes it to the left.
3. The students keep adding a sentence and passing the paper around until you call stop (10-15 minutes should be sufficient).
4. Students open the piece of paper and work in their groups to write a story or poem using the sentences.

Caveats and Options

1. The writing at the end of the game can be done individually or in pairs.

Nikhat Shameem is a lecturer in the Institute of Language Teaching and Learning at the University of Auckland, in New Zealand.

Musical Messages

Levels
Intermediate

Aims
Express preferences,
agreements, and
disagreements
Practice the use of
linking words and
discourse markers to
improve text coherence

Class Time
45–60 minutes

Preparation Time
None

Resources
Overhead projector
(OHP), transparencies
(OHTs), and pens

This game builds on students' interest in and knowledge of popular songs. Working in groups and using the titles of songs, students compose a message and discuss its clarity and coherence. You can then use the text to teach linking words and discourse markers.

Procedure

1. Divide students into groups of four or five. In groups, students brainstorm titles of their 10 favorite songs. If students only know songs in their L1, have them translate the titles into English. You may allow more time for translation, but limit students' brainstorming to 20 minutes.
2. When students have reached agreement on their list, have them copy the titles for the other groups in the class.
3. Collect the lists and distribute copies to the other groups. In short, all groups should have copies of their friends' top 10 hits in addition to their own.
4. Working in groups, students should use as many of the titles as possible to create a message. Remind students that they cannot add words to the titles or change words in them.
5. Have students write the message on a transparency.
6. Stop the activity after 15 minutes. The students exchange their transparencies and count the number of titles used in the message.
7. The group that uses the most titles in their message is the winner.

Caveats and Options

1. After the winner has been declared, display the messages on the OHP. The class will read each message and choose the one they consider most meaningful.

2. You can take the same messages and have the students examine them for coherence. Students can suggest discourse markers and linking words to add to make the message clearer and more coherent.
3. You will need a bank of at least 40 titles to create a meaningful message.

Contributors

Christine C. M. Goh and Cheah Yin Mee are lecturers in the School of Arts, National Institute of Education, Nanyang Technological University, in Singapore. Goh is interested in the teaching of oral communication skills for general and academic purposes. Cheah's interests are in language and literacy education at the primary school level.

◆ Grammar in Discourse
Grid Games

Levels
Any

Aims
Engage in lively
communication
Practice a variety of
language skills and
functions

Class Time
20-60 minutes

Preparation Time
20 minutes

Resources
Prepared set of grids
Dice

In these communicative and versatile games, students roll dice and keep score as they practice grammar, vocabulary, and discourse functions, such as extending invitations, asking for information, making requests or complaints, offering to help, and giving explanations.

Procedure

1. Prepare grids, choosing either the expanded or simplified version as suits your needs. (See Appendixes A and B.)
2. Put students in groups of three to five, providing each group with one grid and one die. Explain the rules of the game as follows:
   ● The first player rolls the die twice. The first roll is for the number at the top of the grid, and the second roll is for the number at the side of the grid.
   ● The square where the two numbers meet describes the task the student must do (e.g., *Tell the group what you did last night*). If the student performs this task to the satisfaction of the other players, the student receives a number of points equal to the two rolls of the die (e.g., a 6 and a 4 would give the student 10 points).
   ● If the task is not performed correctly, the player gets no points, and the game continues with the second player.
3. Call time as appropriate, allowing about 1 hour for the expanded grid and less time for the simplified grid.
4. Have students add up their points and declare winners.

Caveats and Options

1. The grids are extremely versatile. They can be used for a wide variety of tasks, including simple review of irregular verb forms or comparatives. The tasks can be general (e.g., invite someone to a party or ask someone to lend you money) or thematic, such as restaurant functions (e.g., order a dessert or ask for your bill).

162

2. Small prizes can be given to winners. If you use the grids often, you can keep score throughout a semester and award a grand prize to the student who has accumulated the most points. In cases where group members disagree as to whether a player has performed the task satisfactorily, act as the referee to decide challenges.

Appendix A: Sample Expanded Grid

Tell the group a true sentence about yourself. Use the correct verb tense, according to the time cue.

	1	2	3	4	5	6
1	last week	usually	last summer	every morning	tomorrow	yesterday
2	last year	some-times	tomorrow morning	right now	this afternoon	in 1995
3	often	next year	day after tomorrow	next summer	always	next weekend
4	10 years ago	tonight	last night	seldom	on my next birthday	5 years ago
5	last Thanks-giving	rarely	next summer	now	once a week	on my last birthday
6	when I was a child	never	day before yesterday	every Sunday	in 2005	once a month

Appendix B: Sample Simplified Grid

Tell the group a true sentence about yourself. Use the correct verb tense and time cue.

	2 tonight	3 next week	4 in 2005
5 tomorrow	6 after class	7 next month	8 this weekend
9 next year	10 tomorrow morning	11 this summer	12 on Sunday

Acknowledgment

I wish to thank Kevin Cross for his idea for the simplified version of the grid.

Contributor

Sally Winn teaches ESL at City College, San Francisco, in the United States.

Grammar Poker

Levels
Any

Aims
Proofread for typical
ESL/EFL errors

Class Time
10-30 minutes

Preparation Time
10-20 minutes

Resources
Examples of typical
errors
Chalkboard, whiteboard,
or overhead projector
(OHP) and
transparencies (OHTs)
Chalk or pens

S tudents can hone their proofreading skills in this collaborative grammar game.

Procedure

1. Select or create 10-15 sentences, some of which contain errors in grammar and punctuation. Whenever possible, focus on language forms that you are currently discussing in class. Write the first sentence on the chalkboard or whiteboard and ask the students if the sentence is correct. After they respond, you say, "Wanna bet?" Ask them how much money they would be willing to wager that the sentence is right or wrong, and then tell them the answer.
2. Put students in groups of three or four. Assign one student, A, to be the group secretary and ask A to write $500 at the top of a piece of paper.
3. Write the next sentence on the board and ask students to decide whether it is right or wrong. They place a bet (minimum $5, maximum all their money), depending on how certain they feel about their choice. If they guess correctly, they add their wager to their current amount. Conversely, incorrect guesses will cause them to lose their wager.
4. Proceed through the list of sentences in the same way. The group with the most money at the end is the winner.

Caveats and Options

1. The game is played more efficiently when the sentences are on an OHT.
2. I do not include spelling in my Grammar Poker games, but this could be appropriate, depending on the class. Punctuation works well in units that cover reported speech and clauses.

3. If a group loses all its money, it could borrow funds from a benevolent group and pay them back.

Contributor

Dennis Bricault is the director of ESL Programs and an instructor in Spanish at North Park College, in Chicago, Illinois, in the United States. He has 17 years' teaching and administrative experience in Spain, Hungary, and the United States.

Where's Whatsit?

Levels
Any

Aims
Practice the use of
prepositions in a task-
based situation

Class Time
10–15 minutes

Preparation Time
Several seconds

Resources
Small classroom objects
(e.g., rulers, erasers,
pens)

This nonthreatening guessing game is a good way to wrap up a lesson on prepositions.

Procedure

1. Before class begins, place one of the objects on top of something, underneath something, or between two other things.
2. Divide the class into two teams or into groups.
3. Tell the class that they have to identify an object you have chosen in the classroom, using only yes/no questions about position (e.g., "Is it on the wall? Is it behind you?").
4. Teams take turns asking position questions; no points are lost if the answer is incorrect.
5. Either team may try to guess the object at any time, but if they guess wrong, the point goes to the other side.
6. The first team to identify the object wins the point.

Caveats and Options

1. This game works best as a short activity at the end of a class.

Contributor

Peter Roberts is English language project officer with the Ministry of Education, in Singapore.

It's in the Bag

Levels
Beginning +

Aims
Reinforce understanding
of the meanings of
prepositions of location

Class Time
20 minutes

Preparation Time
10 minutes

Resources
Six to eight very small
objects to use as prizes
(e.g., pieces of candy,
pens or pencils, coins)
Chalkboard or
whiteboard and chalk or
pens

This version of the game Hangman uses prepositional phrases in the blanks for letters. It gives students extra motivation to guess and understand the meaning of prepositions because the guessing and comprehension of the prepositional phrase in question produce a reward at the end.

Procedure

1. Hide the six or eight objects around the classroom in various locations that can be easily described by prepositional phrases, such as *behind a book on the shelf above the teacher's desk*, *on one of the file cabinets*, or *between the pages of a red book*.

2. Keeping a record of these locations and the prepositional phrases that describe their location, draw a hangman scaffold on the chalkboard or whiteboard. Underneath it, draw a horizontal line for each letter in the prepositional phrase, leaving spaces between words. For example, spaces would look like this for

   In   the   desk   drawer
   --   ---   ----   ------

3. Tell the class they must guess a prepositional phrase represented by the spaces on the chalkboard or whiteboard. They can only guess the prepositional phrase one letter at a time. If a letter they guess is correct, write it on the chalkboard or whiteboard in the space where it appears in the prepositional phrase. Anyone can try to guess what the prepositional phrase is. If the letter is wrong (i.e., does not appear anywhere in the prepositional phrase or phrases), begin to draw for each incorrect guess the body parts of a person hanging on the

168

scaffold. If you complete an entire body before the class guesses the prepositional phrase, the class loses. (They never do.)

4. Begin the game by letting anyone in the class guess a letter. If the letter they guess is in the phrase, write it in all of the spaces where it appears and let the person who suggested it—or anyone else if that person has no idea—guess what the prepositional phrase is. If the guessed letter is not in the phrase, draw the first body part of the hanging man (head). For the next incorrect guess, draw legs (one at a time), and then arms, feet, and hands.

5. Continue this process until the body is complete—in which case the class has lost the game—or until someone guesses the prepositional phrase. Whoever makes the final correct guess as to the prepositional phrase gets to find the prize in the location suggested by the prepositional phrase.

6. Repeat the procedure until students have guessed all of the prepositional phrases and found all of the prizes.

Contributor

Victoria Holder, an ESL instructor at San Francisco State University and San Francisco City College, in the United States, has recently published a teacher's resource book on practicing grammar without paper.

Who Is It?

Levels
Intermediate +

Aims
Distinguish between
restrictive and
nonrestrictive relative
clauses
Learn to set off
nonrestrictive relative
clauses with commas

Class Time
25 minutes

Preparation Time
None

Resources
Overhead projector
(OHP), chalkboard, or
whiteboard
Overhead transparencies
(OHTs), chalk, or pens

This activity offers a functional way to highlight the differences between restrictive and nonrestrictive relative clauses using contrasting *who* clauses to describe class members.

Procedure

1. Ask three or four different students what country they are from. Then ask if they know where you are from. (In my case, at least some of them know that I am from Canada.)
2. Put sentences on the OHP, chalkboard, or whiteboard instructing the class to point to the student who is from a certain country (e.g., "Point to the student who is from Ethiopia. Point to the student who is from Malaysia. Point to the student who is from Mexico.), and include a nonrestrictive clause about the teacher (e.g., "Point to the teacher, who is from Canada").
3. It is quickly apparent that, to obey the commands about the students, the information in the relative clause helps answer the question, Which one?, and that this is not true for the command about the teacher.
4. Make sure that the students notice that if the relative clauses in the commands about the students are erased, they will not know which student is being referred to; however, if the relative clause in the command about the teacher is erased, they can still point to the teacher.

Caveats and Options

1. You can create similar examples about the classroom, students, or anything the students all know. The only requirement is that the examples be real in the same way that the examples given in this text were real for my class.

2. The difference between restrictive and nonrestrictive relative clauses is relatively easy to illustrate but much harder to explain. For many students, this simple demonstration is quite useful. For example, in writing, the difference between restrictive and nonrestrictive relative clauses is indicated by the punctuation. Restrictive relative clauses are not punctuated; nonrestrictive relative clauses are set off from the rest of the sentence by commas.

Contributor

Graham Thurgood is a professor of linguistics at California State University, in the United States.

Part V: Developing Fluency

Editors' Note

The activities in this section offer students sufficient scaffolding in terms of language and content knowledge that they can concentrate on developing fluency in communicating a message. These games allow students, unconsciously, to integrate known language, subject matter, and discourse skills into an accessible and comprehensible system.

Fluency means that students are able talk or write in the L2 without worrying about accuracy overly much. The activities in this section use various strategies to encourage fluency, including repetition, imitation, rehearsal, and impromptu speech and writing, when the content matter is familiar. It is important that these activities be used only when the learners are wholly familiar with the skills and content matter being practiced, as confidence building is an essential element in encouraging fluency. Fluency-building exercises in this section range from those that revise and review previously acquired language skills to those that enable students to practice known vocabulary items to those that encourage fluency in a content area or help students become more fluent speakers and writers.

◆ Language Skills: Review and Revision

Instant Interview

Levels
Beginning

Aims
Practice question forms
and selected verb tenses

Class Time
5-15 minutes

Preparation Time
5 minutes

Resources
None

This activity is a variation of the tried-and-true student survey, but with the twist that the students control the specific questions.

Procedure

1. Think of a verb tense that you wish to review; a contrast of simple past/present perfect tenses works well as an example.
2. Choose four or five target verbs, preferably irregular. On the board, write a category related to each verb, followed by the base form of the verb:

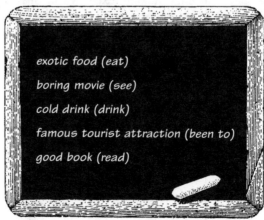

exotic food (eat)

boring movie (see)

cold drink (drink)

famous tourist attraction (been to)

good book (read)

3. Ask students to copy the category and verb, and provide one example for each category (e.g., *an exotic food: octopus*).

176

4. Have students then interview two or three classmates, starting with a question in the present perfect (e.g., "Have you ever eaten octopus?") and following up with a question requiring the simple past (e.g., "When/Where did you eat it? Did you like it? Why/Why not?").
5. Do a brief wrap-up activity by having students report their findings to the class.

Caveats and Options

1. Be creative and use amusing or challenging categories.
2. You can extend the activity to include a short written summary for homework.

Contributor

Dennis Bricault is the director of ESL programs and an instructor in Spanish at North Park College in Chicago, Illinois, in the United States. He has 17 years' teaching and administrative experience in Spain, Hungary, and the United States.

Fortune Tellers

Levels
High beginning-low
intermediate

Aims
Practice simple past,
present, future, and
present continuous verb
tenses
Practice and develop
culturally relevant
vocabulary
Experience
communication in an
enjoyable, supportive
atmosphere

Class Time
30 minutes

Preparation Time
30–45 minutes to
organize realia

Resources
Stack of large index or
file cards (one card per
student) with pictures
from popular,
contemporary
magazines

As fortune tellers, students develop their own interpretations and predictions about people and events, focusing on the verb tense they must use to deliver fortunes. The use of pictures from popular magazines introduces students to relevant cultural images and allows them to increase their vocabulary. Communication takes place between students as they agree, disagree, comment on, and laugh at one another's imaginary pasts, presents, and futures.

Procedure

1. Ask students to sit opposite one another, in two rows, across a narrow table or in concentric circles of chairs.
2. Give each student a different picture depicting a variety of situations, family settings, social settings, employment settings, locations, vehicles, clothing, modes of travel, or animals. The student holds the same picture during the entire session.
3. Direct the students on the right side of the table (or sitting in the inside circle) to tell the fortune of the partner facing them, using the partner's picture as a reference. Be explicit about whether they are to tell the past, present, or future.
4. After 3 minutes, direct the partners to switch roles. After the partners have told each other's fortunes, each student moves one space to the right, and the students on the ends now move to the other side of the table. Repeat Steps 2 and 3 until you feel students have had sufficient practice with the targeted tense or tenses.
5. You can change verb tense focus at any time by directing the fortune tellers to talk about their partner's present or predict their partner's future.

Caveats and Options

1. In preparing the cards for this activity, use pictures from stories or advertisements depicting a variety of social settings, objects, institutions, people at work and play, and scenery. The use of impersonal visuals—rather than family photographs, for example—keeps an important safe distance between personal realities and linguistic practice.
2. You may use the visuals as a starting point for group discussion of relevant cultural and personal issues.
3. Direct students on the right to tell the past and the students on the left to tell the future. As they move around the table, they will have an opportunity to work with each tense.
4. This activity works best with 10 students (five pairs). It is not as much fun with only six students.
5. This activity could be done while sitting in two facing rows or concentric circles on the floor.
6. The game can stop whenever you feel that the students have had enough practice or that their interest is waning. It is not essential that each student interact with everyone else.
7. You can return to this activity another day when students are ready to practice verb tenses again.

Contributor

Maggie Warbey teaches ESL and applied linguistics theory in the Department of Linguistics at the University of Victoria, in Canada. Her advanced-level text, The Write Way, *was published by Harcourt Brace, Canada, in 1996.*

Shop Until You Drop

Level
High beginning–
intermediate

Aims
Practice countable and
uncountable nouns
Learn appropriate
counters for products
Improve memory skills

Class Time
Variable

Preparation Time
None

Resources
Picture or flash cards
(optional)
Examples of counters
(e.g., cartons, bottles)
(optional)

The English system of countable and uncountable nouns and using markers or counters for these nouns can be confusing for students. This exercise is an enjoyable way for them to practice a variety of structures in a simple game.

Procedure

1. Seat the students in a formation where they can all see each other, such as a horseshoe shape or circle. Explain how to play the game.
2. For the first demonstration the teacher will be the leader. Start with, "I'm going to go shopping and I'm going to buy two bottles of wine." The next person repeats, "I'm going to go shopping and I'm going to buy two bottles of wine and . . . ," and names an item. The next person repeats the previous information. The game proceeds until a student cannot repeat all the previous items.
3. Start with a new leader from the next person. Continue the game for as long as you wish.

Caveats and Options

1. The game can be adapted to include all kinds of counters or items. It could be included in a shopping lesson as a practice or review of what has been taught.
2. Students do not have to say, "I'm going to go shopping and I'm going to buy . . . ." You may omit this part or substitute something else that you feel is appropriate.

Contributor

Sarah Berg, originally from Australia, is currently teaching in Tokyo, Japan, where she has been living and working since 1988.

Picture This!

Levels
Beginning-intermediate

Aims
Retain vocabulary
Review or reinforce a
particular grammatical
structure in a
communicative situation

Class Time
Variable

Preparation Time
1 hour

Resources
Magazine pictures
mounted on cardboard
or large colored paper
Plain paper
Chalkboard or
whiteboard and chalk or
pens
Small colored paper
squares for use as
markers

This game helps students develop listening, speaking, and writing skills, and can reinforce any lesson dealing with verb forms. It allows students to practice particular, repetitive structures, yet is not boring. It also gives them the opportunity to enrich their range of vocabulary (e.g., for a picture of a man sitting on a chair, appropriate verb alternatives might be *sit*, *sit down*, or *relax*).

Procedure

1. Collect at least 25 pictures that can illustrate a particular structure. Model several pictures or all of them, depending on the difficulty of the vocabulary involved. For example, if students are studying the present continuous tense in combination with possessive adjectives, you could hold up the picture and ask, "What are they doing?" Students would respond, "They're washing their hands."
2. Once the pattern is established, a student volunteer holds up a picture and asks the question. As students respond, place a telegraphic version of one of their answers on the chalkboard or whiteboard (e.g., *they/wash/hands*), and continue to do this for each picture until all the pictures have been shown.
3. At this point, students take a sheet of paper and fold it in threes and in threes again so that it has nine boxes.
4. Have students write a sentence in each box. For the example in Steps 2 and 3, they would use the present continuous tense with a possessive adjective to form nine different statements based on the pictures and cue words on the chalkboard or whiteboard.
5. Begin the game. Initially you call out the questions, and then the winner of the first game calls them out, and so on. Distribute the markers, shuffle the pictures, and place them face down on the desk.

6. Pick up each picture and ask the class or individual to reply. For example, you could hold up a picture and ask, "What's he doing?" Students could reply, "He's brushing his teeth."
7. The students with this statement on their paper cover it with a marker. The game proceeds until a student has covered all nine boxes, at which point he calls out, "Winner!"
8. The student who claimed he'd won must then read his statements out loud as the caller verifies them by checking the pictures. After checking, that student is then proclaimed the winner and becomes the next caller.

Caveats and Options

1. Advise the students to choose at random—not just the first nine cryptic versions they see on the chalkboard. Also, check students' papers to see that sentences are grammatically and semantically correct before the game begins.
2. If there is a tie, or in the event of multiple winners, each winner can pick a statement (in the earlier example, a present continuous statement), and the caller picks up pictures until one comes up that matches a contestant's statement. That student is then the winner.
3. In the unusual event there are only two pictures left and no student has yet won, the game is a stalemate, as there will be multiple winners if all pictures are shown.
4. To sustain interest, there can be two winners for each game. After a student wins, the caller can continue picking up pictures until a second student has won.
5. An alternative is to organize the class into two teams for a world championship. The first team to win four games is the champion.
6. Use pictures that are unambiguous and can be seen at a distance. Mounting the pictures on cardboard or large colored paper will make them easier to handle and will preserve them longer.

Appendix: Sample Student Game Card

They're washing their hands.	He's sleeping in his bed.	They're writing in their books.
He's eating his dinner.	She's combing her hair.	He's driving his car.
She's reading a book.	They're riding their bicycles.	He's brushing his teeth.

Contributor

Judith Book-Ehrlichman, specialist in curriculum/materials development, teaches ESL at Bergen Community College, in New Jersey, in the United States.

◆ Developing Fluency With Vocabulary

Let's Go Shopping

Levels
Beginning

Aims
Practice requesting,
offering, and receiving
shopping items

Class Time
30 minutes

Preparation Time
30 minutes

Resources
Chart with pictures of
merchandise
Individual pictures of
the merchandise
Low partition

Two teams work against the clock in this buying and selling game. An element of reality is added by the fact that the shoppers cannot see what the sellers are offering, and have a genuine reason for asking, "Do you have . . . ?"

Procedure

1. Collect or draw pictures of items to offer for sale. These can be vocabulary items already familiar to the students or items that you wish to teach or reinforce. Make a chart of these images and then copy it. Cut the copy into individual pictures of the merchandise.
2. Divide the class into two groups, buyers (Team A) and sellers (Team B). Team A sits on one side of a low partition while Team B sits on the other side. Give Team A the chart with all the items on it, and give Team B five of the items to sell.
3. A member from Team A asks if Team B has an item (i.e., "Do you have . . . ?"). A member of Team B replies, "Certainly. Here you are" or, "Sorry, we don't have any today."
4. Team A members take turns requesting items, trying to identify the five items that Team B has for sale. You can set a time limit, noting the number of items identified within that limit or the time it took A to buy all five items.
5. Have the teams reverse roles in the next round, with Team A acting as the sellers and Team B as the buyers. Compare Team B's time or number of items with Team A's. Depending on the time available, a few rounds can be played, and the quickest team or the team who bought the most items is the winner.

Caveats and Options

1. Different or more difficult request and offering forms can be reinforced in this game. Adapt the language to the ability of your students.
2. With larger classes, make more copies of the merchandise chart and divide the class into more buyer and seller groups who can play simultaneously.
3. At a later stage, you could give the students money and have them practice asking and giving prices.

Contributor

Geraldine Hetherton is an EFL lecturer at Fukui Prefectural University, in Japan, and has also taught in Europe, Africa, and the Middle East.

Dice Game

Levels
Low intermediate +

Aims
Creative practice and
revision of vocabulary

Class Time
15–30 minutes

Preparation Time
5 minutes (after the die
is prepared)

Resources
Large game die
Vocabulary list with the
target words
Timers (optional)

This is a highly motivating activity in which students act out, draw, or describe to one another recently learned vocabulary.

Procedure

1. One student sits in a chair facing the group and rolls the game die. There are a number of possibilities, depending on the roll of the die. If the die says
   - *draw* or *act* or *describe*, the student chooses a word from the vocabulary list and follows the command, and the rest of the group has 2 or 3 minutes to guess the word
   - *draw, act, or describe*, the student can choose one of these options
   - *group acts* or *group describes*, the student has 2 or 3 minutes to guess while the group carries out the command
2. Each person in the group should have a turn at the front.
3. The winner is the person who guesses the most correct words.

Caveats and Options

1. The game works well as a competition between two teams. In this case, one student from each team sits at the front, directing the team's descriptions, acting, or drawings. The contestants change when the time is up or when a team guesses the word. The team with the most correctly guessed words wins.
2. You could write the words in advance on small pieces of paper, placing them in a pile face down on a table, rather than supplying them from a list.

186

3. You could also introduce two game dice. The teams can work off the same or separate lists or piles of words. Separate timers will need to be assigned to each team.

Appendix: Constructing the Game Dice

The game dice need to be big enough (at least 1 sq in, or 7 sq cm) for all students to see the writing. You can make them from a wooden cube or from cardboard. If you construct a cardboard cube, be sure to use heavy card and allow tabs around the outside for gluing.

The commands for the six faces of the die are as follows:

1. Draw
2. Describe
3. Act
4. Draw, describe, or act
5. Group describes
6. Group acts

Contributor

Graeme Smith is teaching in Auckland, New Zealand, and has just completed an MA in language teaching at the University of Auckland.

Pack It In

Levels
Intermediate

Aims
Practice communicative
functions of guessing
and estimating
Confirm or reject
guesses

Class Time
40 minutes

Preparation Time
None

Resources
Paper
Pen or pencil

This game helps students focus on its content, taking their attention away from the structures they are practicing. At the same time, it allows them repeated practice of certain intermediate-level language structures that can be applied and used in real-life situations. Using context imaginatively, students generate realistic language samples. Eager to successfully complete this game, students will likely move beyond the targeted language to practice other known structures.

Procedure

1. Have students envision a scenario for which they need 10 specific items. For example, one student envisions packing a suitcase for a trip to Hawaii. One thinks of shopping for ingredients to make a spaghetti dinner. One plans to fill her backpack for a day hike.
2. Ask students to describe their scenario at the top of a piece of paper and list the 10 items underneath. For example, the student packing for Hawaii might list *swimsuit, towel, shorts, a book*, and so on.
3. Working in pairs, students perform the following: One student tells the other his scenario, and the other student guesses the items needed for the scenario.

Caveats and Options

1. This game is designed for repeated practice of specific language structures. You should write these on the chalkboard or whiteboard and practice them before the game begins (see the Appendix).
2. If students have not successfully guessed each other's items, you can open the guessing to the class. State the scenario for the class, and see if they can guess the remaining items.

References and Further Reading

Folse, K. S. (1993). *Talk a lot*. Ann Arbor, MI: University of Michigan Press.

Sion, C. (Ed.). (1983). *Recipes for tired teachers*. White Plains, NY: Addison-Wesley Longman.

Appendix: Sample Language Structures

I bet you have a . . . / I bet there's a . . .
You probably have a . . .
I think you brought/packed/included a . . .
You'd need a . . .
You're right, I do have a . . .
No, but you're close. It's the same size/shape/color.
No, I don't have any [X] (e.g., swimming) things. I don't like to [X].
Give me a hint.
What's it used for?

Contributor

Lynn Stafford-Yilmaz teaches ESL and coordinates sites for the American Cultural Exchange in Seattle, Washington, in the United States.

Communication Unplugged

Levels
Intermediate +

Aims
Practice vocabulary and
compensatory
communication
strategies in a
communicative context

Class Time
30 minutes

Preparation Time
5–15 minutes

Resources
Cards with a word or
phrase written on them
Timer
Means of keeping score

This highly interactive game requires students to quickly think on their feet in order to describe common words, phrases, or vocabulary used in daily conversation.

Procedure

1. Create two teams, designating a speaker for each team. There will be a different speaker in each round.
2. Place a stack of word or phrase cards in front of the speaker for the first team. Set the timer for 90 seconds, and start.
3. The speaker describes, defines, or explains the word or phrase on the top card until the team members guess it.
4. If the first team guesses the word or phrase, the speaker should immediately give the remainder of the stack of cards to the speaker from the other team. This carries on until the timer goes off. At this point, the team stuck with the stack loses the round, and the other team receives 1 point. The other team begins the next round.
5. If the first team does not guess the word or phrase within the 90 seconds, the other team gets a point. The other team begins the next round.
6. The game continues until 30 minutes is up. The team with the most points wins.

Caveats and Options

1. The commercial game, Catch Phrases (by Parker Brothers) may be used. If so, you may have to choose certain word or phrase cards appropriate for the students' levels.
2. You may want to point out that this game gives students vocabulary reinforcements, while also allowing them to practice compensatory strategies for communication, such as describing or defining or

explaining, in order to avoid dictionary use in the course of conversation, when pronunciation is not comprehensible or an appropriate word cannot be recalled.

References and Further Reading

Nunan, D. (1989). *Designing tasks for the communicative classroom*. Cambridge: Cambridge University Press.

Contributor

Susan M. Barone is language specialist in the English for Internationals Department at Vanderbilt University, in the United States.

◆ Capitalizing on Content
Human Bingo

Levels
Intermediate +

Aims
Practice simple question
and answer techniques
Exchange information in
an affective classroom
atmosphere

Class Time
20 minutes

Preparation Time
15 minutes

Resources
Game sheets

This game is used as an icebreaker at the first class meeting. By asking each other questions in a friendly atmosphere, students can make real use of English to communicate with each other. They practice listening and simple question and answer skills, and use the language to talk about themselves, a topic they are already familiar with.

Procedure

1. Design a bingo sheet with as many squares as you like, preferably 16 or 25.
2. Ask students to sit in a big circle and get a pen ready.
3. Distribute the bingo sheet; ask students to put their names in the center square because this will help to identify the winner and increase students' chances of winning the game.
4. Go over the rules of the game briefly:
   - Look for people who may sign their names in the squares.
   - Try to fill out all the spaces.
   - Each name cannot appear more than two times.
   - Count 5 points for each full line (vertical, horizontal, or diagonal).
   - The person who has accumulated the most points at the end of the game wins.
5. Start the game. Ask students to walk around and ask each other questions (see Appendix A) about the topics on their bingo sheets. Students sign the squares if they can answer the question affirmatively. It is better to allow two signatures per box so that students can talk to more new friends.

6. Allow 10 minutes for the question and answer part, adjusting the time to suit the mood of the class.
7. When time is up, collect all the bingo sheets.
8. Tell students you are going to check the signatures on some squares to make sure there is no cheating. This is a chance to invite students to speak more about themselves. For example:

Teacher: Let's see who has won a prize. Helen, you did. Can you tell us what you have got?

Teacher: Playing a musical instrument . . . Martin and Heather can play musical instruments. Heather, perhaps you can tell us about the instrument you play.

Caveats and Options

1. This game can be adapted to suit different teaching purposes by designing appropriate cues for the questions. For example, practice asking questions in the simple past tense, beginning with "Is . . . ?"
2. Beginning-level students may need help forming correct questions. You may write question openers on the board to help or do some simple revision activity first. Examples include:

Can you . . . ?
Do you . . . ?
Are you . . . ?
Have you . . . ?

Appendix A: Sample Bingo Sheet

In this game, you must
1. look for people who may sign their names in the squares
2. try to fill in all the spaces.
3. make sure a name does not appear more than two times
4. count 5 points for each full line

The person who has accumulated the most points at the end of the game will be the winner.

has been to Disneyland	can use a computer	likes swimming	is wearing jeans
can speak French	has a birthday this month	has visited the school library	can play a musical instrument
has a part-time job	can roll her tongue	your name	is wearing contact lenses
has won a prize	has visited five or more	keeps a pet at home	likes singing

Contributor

Pauline Tam is a lecturer in the English Department at the City University of Hong Kong.

Exchanging Learning Strategies

Levels
Intermediate +

Aims
Learn communicative
strategies
Develop autonomy

Class Time
1 hour

Preparation Time
None

Resources
Extracts from a suitable
book

In this activity students gain knowledge of learning strategies and fluency in a content area by discussing, repeating, and reporting on the information given.

Procedure

1. Make available short extracts from a book for students on learner strategies (see References and Further Reading).
2. Students work in groups of three or four, with everyone in one group reading the same extract. After reading silently or aloud, students discuss what they have read, using prompt questions from the board. For example:
   - What exactly is the writer saying?
   - What new ideas does it give you?
   - Have you tried anything like this?
3. Give each person in the group a number. Have students form new groups corresponding to the numbers they have just received.
4. In these new groups, each person reports on the strategy they have already discussed. Remind students that this book is available in the library or bookshop.

References and Further Reading

Rubin, J., & Thompson, I. (1994). *How to be a more successful language learner.* Boston: Heinle & Heinle.

Contributor

Marilyn Lewis is a senior lecturer at the Institute for Language Teaching and Learning, at the University of Auckland, in New Zealand.

The Social Game

Levels
Intermediate +

Aims
Gain fluency through exchange of ideas, feelings, and experiences on favorite topics
Practice interviewing and note-taking skills
Practice writing and delivering a speech

Class Time
Two class periods, with the second on the following class day

Preparation Time
15 minutes

Resources
One different interview question, written on a strip of paper, for each student
Appropriate mood music

This fluency-building activity helps students prepare for the social game of mixing with and talking to a variety of people while discovering interesting insights about them.

Procedure

1. Introduce the activity to the students by explaining that they are going to learn more about each other through interviews, for exchange of ideas, feelings, and experiences on favorite topics.
2. Explain that students will give a short speech on their interviews on the following day.
3. Set the scene by having students imagine that they are going to talk to people as if they were at a party and therefore feel obligated to keep the conversation going in a slick, active, and interesting manner, so as not to lose a golden opportunity to make someone's acquaintance. (Make the students aware of ways and techniques of keeping the conversation going on a certain topic by frequently using wh- and related questions.)
4. Divide the class into pairs and give each student a different interview topic. Ask the students to memorize their topic and collect the papers 2 or 3 minutes later.
5. Have students interview three to five different people, in changing pairs, on their topic. Before starting the interviews, remind the students to jot down the main points of each conversation while keeping the conversation lively and eliciting a maximum amount of information on the topic to discover more about their partners' lives and personalities. Let the students know that you will tell them when to change partners.

6. During the interviews, play appropriate music to facilitate a pleasant atmosphere.
7. After the interviews, explain to the students how to prepare a short speech to report to the class the results of their interviews.
8. Explain that the person who reports the most information in the best manner will be judged as the winner in the social game.

Appendix: Sample Topics

Following are some sample questions that students can answer and compare with their classmates. They must be prepared to give reasons for their answers.

What is one book you would like to take with you on a trip around the world and why?

What famous person would you like to have dinner with and why?

What kind of person would you like to marry? If you are already married, what kind of person would you like your son or daughter to marry?

What are the two most important qualities in your life? Why?

Where in the world would you most like to spend your next holiday?

As a small child, what was your favorite pastime?

Who is your favorite relative? Describe that person.

As a small child, who was your best friend? Describe that person.

What would you do if you suddenly inherited a million dollars?

Which pair of shoes give you the happiest memories? Why?

What is the most beautiful sight that you have ever seen?

What is the biggest achievement in your life?

Who has helped you most in your life? Describe this person and what he or she did.

What was the funniest experience in your life?

References and Further Reading

Moskowitz, G. (1978). *Caring and sharing in the foreign language class: A sourcebook on humanistic techniques*. Rowley, MA: Newbury House.

Contributor

Elizabeth Lange teaches at Temple University Japan.

Memory Mix

Levels
Intermediate +

Aims
Finish the last class on a positive note through exchange of memorable, funny, interesting, or unusual things that happened during the semester

Class Time
Up to 1 hour

Preparation Time
None

Resources
None

This activity is a highly interactive way of saying good-bye on the last day of class. It allows students to practice known structures and vocabulary as they recall some happy classroom moments. Repetition is an essential element of this activity.

Procedure

1. Have everyone write on a small piece of paper one or two funny, interesting, or out-of-the-ordinary things that happened in class during the semester. Ask everyone to pick moments that they know their classmates could recall with some memory prodding.
2. Demonstrate ways to spur someone's memory about something. Introduce such questions or statements as "Who made everyone scream when they . . . ?" "What were you thinking when you saw . . . ?" "Everyone almost jumped out of their seats when . . . " Follow these with responses (e.g., "Oh, that's right!" or "Yes, I remember I felt shocked . . . ." or "Oh, wasn't that funny!").
3. Ask students to sustain a conversation on and around the topic for several minutes, recalling associated feelings, emotions, reactions, or any related memories and what it meant to them.
4. After partners have enjoyed talking to each other on their topics, they should exchange papers with each other and find another partner.
5. Tell the students to circulate around the room until they have talked, exchanged papers, said good-bye to everyone, and confirmed phone numbers.
6. Then ask all the students to stand up, find a partner, and start the ball rolling on their topics.

Contributor

Elizabeth Lange teaches English at Temple University Japan.

◆ Sharpening Speaking
Don't Say It

Levels
Any

Aims
Gain fluency with
already acquired
language in a
nonstressful
communicative situation

Class Time
10 minutes +

Preparation Time
None

Resources
Clock (optional)

This communication game challenges students to use their English communication skills in a competition. Beginners focus on simple question-and-answer dialogues, while more advanced students converse at a higher level. Because correctly responding to one another is a key component, students actively monitor one another.

Procedure

1. Pair off students.
2. Explain that each student must try to make his partner say *no* while being careful not to say *no* himself. Have them keep a tally of the number of times *no* is said by the partner. After 5 minutes, the student with the lowest score wins.

Caveats and Options

1. In addition to no and yes, a head nod for yes and a head shake for no could be included in prohibited forms of communication.
2. Beginners take turns questioning one another and time how long it takes for their partners to say no.
3. With highly competitive students, semifinal and final matches could be held.

David Hirsh is an ESL teacher currently working at Assumption University, in Bangkok, Thailand.

Contributor

The *Stop!* Game

Levels
Beginning +

Aims
Develop questioning
skills and quick
responses

Class Time
Up to 1 hour

Preparation Time
30 minutes

Resources
Short narrative passage,
typed on a page with
10 comprehension
questions at the bottom

This noisy game helps students think quickly on a topic that they explore and then speak on quickly in English.

Procedure

1. Have students form a circle so that everyone is the same distance from you. Students listen to a short passage while you read it aloud. Read it a couple of times and then ask some general questions to check comprehension.
2. Give each student a copy of the passage with some questions at the bottom of the sheet. Ask them to answer the questions without looking at the passage. When they finish, they can check their own answers.
3. Pair students and have them ask and answer these questions with their partner. The person answering should not look at their written responses. Encourage quick responses, and when they seem ready, have partners continue without looking at their papers at all.
4. When they know the questions and can ask and answer well, have each pair write 10 more questions. They should only look at the passage while they are writing their questions. As they finish, repeat the exercise, and then change pairs.
5. Now the game begins: Tell the students to put their papers out of sight. Explain that you are going to read the passage as quickly as you can, but if you finish within 5 minutes, you are going to give the students some terrible punishment, such as an extra homework task. The way they will stop you from finishing the passage too quickly is by saying "Stop," and asking you a question that you must answer.

6. When they understand the instructions, tell students to say *stop* as loudly as they can. Go around the group and practice this until everyone says it very loud.
7. Now begin reading quickly!

Caveats and Options

1. Choose a passage that is not too difficult for the group. This is important. The idea is not to stretch their comprehension powers but to encourage quick thinking and responses.
2. This game may be played with students of any level. With high-level students, omit the question formation activities and only answer questions that are grammatically correct.
3. The game may be varied or extended by having a student read and answer the questions, or by having the students work in pairs reading, asking, and answering.
4. Although, at first, the questions should relate to the passage, after a while you can encourage questions designed to prompt imagination.

Contributor

Sonia Millett works for the Corporate Education Program at Temple University Japan.

The Minute Game

Levels
Beginning–intermediate

Aims
Practice speaking at
increased speech rates
Decode English spoken
at faster speech rates

Class Time
15 minutes

Preparation Time
None

Resources
Pair of cymbals
Watch

This game provides an opportunity for beginning- and intermediate-level students to practice increasing the pace of their own oral English delivery and decoding the rapid speech of others.

Procedure

1. Ask a confident student to come to the front of the class. This student must be prepared to answer a number of questions without using the words *yes* or *no*.
2. Ask another student to be the timekeeper. This student must have a watch with a second hand on it and will be responsible for timing the game (1 minute for each game).
3. Ask a third student to be the cymbal clasher. This student is responsible for immediately clashing the cymbals if the student answering the questions says yes or no.
4. Ask the timekeeper to indicate when the questioner can begin.
5. The questioner begins firing questions at the answerer (e.g., "Do you live in a flat? Have you got any brothers and sisters? Do you like going to the cinema? Have you got a boyfriend?") The student answering the questions must reply promptly but without saying yes or no (e.g., "I do; I have two brothers and one sister; I like going to the cinema; I don't have a boyfriend"). If the student answering the question slips up and replies using *yes* or *no*, the student with the cymbals should immediately clash them, and the answering student will have to sit down. If the answering student does not say yes or no and the minute is up, the answering student has won.
6. Demonstrate the game a few times and then ask students to form groups of four. In their groups, the students take turns being

questioner, answerer, timekeeper, and hand clapper (in place of the cymbals). They then play the game four times.

Caveats and Options

1. Emphasize that questions must be asked in rapid succession in order to trick the answerer into saying either yes or no.
2. Stress that prompt replies must be given or else the answerer will be disqualified.
3. Before playing the game, give students practice in inventing alternative answers to yes or no.
4. Before playing the game, elicit a number of questions that can be asked during the game. For beginners, you may wish to limit each game to 30 or 45 seconds.

Contributor

Dino Mahoney is an associate professor in the English Department of the City University of Hong Kong. He has also taught ESL/EFL in England, Greece, and the United Arab Emirates.

Identifying the Differences

This game allows students to interact freely with one another in an interesting context. With its problem-solving element, the game can also enhance students' sense of satisfaction and achievement.

Levels
Intermediate +

Aims
Practice language functions in a communicative manner

Class Time
30 minutes

Preparation Time
10 minutes

Resources
Pictures

Procedure

1. Collect pictures from newspapers, magazines, and books. Photocopy the pictures. Make some alterations to the duplicated ones.
2. Pair off students. Give each pair one set of pictures (one original and one duplicated with alterations).
3. Ask each pair to compare the set of pictures and identify the differences (e.g., number, areas). Have pairs swap sets of pictures when they have finished their own and repeat task.

Caveats and Options

1. The game is designed for students who have a command of some language functions. For students of a more elementary level, some initial practice of the useful language expressions will be necessary beforehand.

Contributor

Teresa Loh is a lecturer in the Department of English, City University of Hong Kong.

◆ Working With Writing
Moving Pictures

Levels
Any

Aims
Contextualize dialogue

Class Time
30–40 minutes

Preparation Time
30 minutes

Resources
Enough copies of story lines so that there is one for each pair

This drama game allows learners to generate their own dialogues from a sequential frame of reference, where each part of the dialogue is connected to a larger narrative. It is designed to actively involve students with the language they are using and to allow them to observe and discuss how their classmates use the language.

Procedure

1. Give out copies of a simple story line, such as the one in the Appendix. Assign each part of the story to pairs of students.
2. Have each pair write a very brief dialogue derived from the assigned story line dialogue. Students practice their dialogue until they can say it without looking at their scripts.
3. Discuss with students the appropriateness of the language used to act out the different language functions. Revise as necessary. Have the pairs act out their stories.

Caveats and Options

1. This game helps to contextualize, in a controlled practice setting, a number of routines that exemplify basic language functions. It can be used in many different ways depending on the students' levels. At the beginning level, you will probably play a major part in the discussion of the appropriateness of language, including body language. At more advanced levels and with fewer students, pairs may combine more than one element of the story. You may want to have students move beyond representing one element of the story to acting out the whole story as a pair.
2. Alternatively, especially in a class of large numbers, students not acting out the story could be asked to observe certain features of the interaction (e.g., body language, levels of politeness, levels of distance).

Appendix: Sample Story Line

Two people pass each other on the street
X dropts his/her wallet/purse
Y picks it up and call X back
X returns and thanks Y
X invites Y for coffee
Y agrees
X and Y introduce each other and ask questions
X invites Y out for a date
Y refuses politely
X invites Y out for a date again
Y refuses less politely
X leaves Y

References and Further Reading

Maley, A., & Duff, A. (1982). *Drama techniques in language learning*. Cambridge: Cambridge University Press.

Scher, A., & Verrall, C. (1987). *Another 100+ ideas for drama*. London: Heinemann Educational Books.

Contributor

Dominic Cogan is a lecturer at Fukui Prefectural University, in Japan.

The Silent Conversation

Levels
Beginning

Aims
Develop quick questions and responses

Class Time
30 minutes +

Preparation Time
5 minutes

Resources
Big pile of paper for writing notes

Even though this game is silent, it engenders a lot of enthusiasm and energy and develops conversation skills in an unusual way.

Procedure

1. Push enough desks together to make a big table. Sit with the students around the table. Everyone needs a pen or pencil. Put a pile of note paper in the middle of the table.
2. Explain that everyone has to write notes to classmates and then deliver them. The notes must contain a question. Recipients must answer the question and ask another. To illustrate this process, write an example:

> Dear Tomoko,
>   The vacation starts next week. What are your plans?
> Well, Bye,
>   Sonia

3. Keep writing, and make sure that everyone else is writing. If you notice a student is not getting any letters, write to that student.
4. Soon everyone will have so many notes to answer or questions they want to ask that they will be sorry when the bell goes.

Caveats and Options

1. This game may be played in a computer lab using e-mail if you have the facilities.

Contributor

Sonia Millett works for the Corporate Education Program at Temple University Japan.

Round-Robin Writing

Levels
Intermediate

Aims
Write a collaborative story in a group
Develop fluency in writing and speaking through repetition

Class Time
30 minutes +

Preparation Time
None

Resources
One piece of paper for each group of four or five students

This activity is an enjoyable way for learners to develop fluency in reading aloud and writing.

Procedure

1. Place students in groups of four or five, giving each group a piece of paper.
2. One member of the group writes a sentence, reads it aloud to the group, and passes the paper to the person on the left. The person who gets the paper adds a sentence to the first sentence, reads both sentences aloud, and passes the paper to the left.
3. Each person getting the paper adds a sentence and reads the contents of the story so far. The group members keep adding a sentence and reading aloud until you call for the last round, when the group has to conclude the story. The last person to add a sentence reads the story aloud.
4. The story is then put away, and each student rewrites the story in his own words.

Caveats and Options

1. Instead of rewriting the story at the end, students can retell their story orally to members of other groups.

Contributor

Nikhat Shameem is a lecturer in the Institute of Language Teaching and Learning, at the University of Auckland, in New Zealand.

Clarifying Arguments

Levels
Intermediate +

Aims
Develop brainstorming
and planning skills for
essay writing

Class Time
15 minutes +

Preparation Time
5 minutes

Resources
Chalkboard or
whiteboard
Chalk or pens

This activity can be used as a warm-up exercise prior to writing an argumentative or discussion essay. It works as a brainstorming activity, helping students to generate ideas, clarify their point of view, develop their powers of persuasion, and present a balanced argument.

Procedure

1. Write a proposition on the board that allows for opposing points of view (e.g., *Smoking should be banned in all public places*).
2. Pair off the students, assigning the letters A and B to each pair.
3. Ask all the A students to spend 3 minutes thinking of all the reasons they can to support the proposition; ask all B students to think of reasons against the proposition.
4. The A students then have 3 minutes to tell their partners their arguments in support of the proposition. The B students can spend 3 minutes giving their arguments against the proposition. Each pair needs to decide which point of view was more effectively supported.
5. Students can then repeat the procedure with a new partner, getting exposure to more ideas and strengthening their own arguments.
6. Students can use the ideas as a springboard for planning and writing an argumentative essay on the same topic.

Caveats and Options

1. This activity works best when you control the timing carefully.
2. It is also possible to use a 4-3-2 format with this activity when students move to new partners. Reduce the amount of time given for students to express their opinions from 4 minutes to 3 and then 2. Restricting the time means that the students have to clarify their ideas and present them as succinctly as possible.

3. Instead of having written outcomes, use this activity as a brainstorming exercise in preparation for a class debate.

Contributor

Fiona Hyland is a senior instructor in the language center at Lingnan College, in Hong Kong.

Also available from TESOL

*New Ways of Using Drama and
Literature in Language Teaching*
Valerie Whiteson, Editor

New Ways of Using Computers in Language Teaching
Tim Boswood, Editor

*Reading and Writing in More Than One Language:
Lessons for Teachers*
Elizabeth Franklin, Editor

Tasks for Independent Language Learning
David Gardner and Lindsay Miller, Editors

Teaching in Action: Case Studies From Second Language Classrooms
Jack C. Richards, Editor

For more information, contact

Teachers of English to Speakers of Other Languages, Inc.
1600 Cameron Street, Suite 300
Alexandria, Virginia 22314 USA
Tel. 703-836-0774 • Fax 703-836-7864
e-mail publ@tesol.edu
http://www.tesol.edu/